COACHING THIRD

COACHING THIRD

THE KEITH LECLAIR STORY

Bethany Bradsher

Whitecaps Media
Houston

Whitecaps Media
Houston, Texas
www.whitecapsmedia.com

Coaching Third: The Keith LeClair Story
© 2010 Lynn LeClair
All rights reserved

ISBN: 978-0-9826353-0-8

CONTENTS

Foreword

COACHING THIRD, IN BASEBALL TERMS, WAS THE LITERAL position where you would find Keith LeClair when his team was at bat. The third base coach's box was where he felt most comfortable. He was giving signs and sending runners home. He was in the game!

While the third base coach's box may have been his position, this in no way represented the ranking of baseball in his life. Baseball was his passion, and it influenced every aspect of his life.

The day Keith was diagnosed with amyotrophic lateral sclerosis (ALS), life as he and our family knew it came to an abrupt halt. There was no five-year plan, ten-year plan, or retirement plan. The plan was to make it day to day.

Amidst our devastation, I personally began to see a remarkable change take place in Keith. He began to immerse himself in Scripture, seek God, and grow spiritually in a way that I had never witnessed. In the life previously dominated by baseball, Christ quickly took the lead. It was Christ and Christ alone who could make sense of this devastation. "Coaching third" also represents the realignment of priorities as Keith faced the greatest challenge of his life; Christ first, family second, and coaching third.

My prayer is that as you read Keith's story, your heart will remain open, that you will think about your own priorities, and that you will be blessed. I hope that you will give this coach one last opportunity to send the runner home. Only this time, the runner must go by way of the cross.

Lynn LeClair
December 2009

Coach LeClair throws batting practice prior to a game against Tennessee at the 2001 NCAA Super Regional tournament in Kinston, N.C.

1

Kinston

NONE OF THEM HAD EVER COME THIS CLOSE. THEY WERE members of the team that many said was the best East Carolina University baseball had ever fielded, even though several players were walk-ons and few were recruited by major programs. Their ultimate destination, with just one team standing in the way, was Omaha, permanent site of the College World Series (CWS). And the Pirates were just two victories removed from that goal, facing the Tennessee Volunteers in nearby Kinston, North Carolina, as the higher seed and the host team.

After a heady victory in the NCAA Regional just six days earlier, the ECU baseball players were starting to give intellectual assent to what looked obvious on paper: They had a real shot at competing in Omaha's hallowed Rosenblatt Stadium as one of the top eight teams in the nation.

Standing just behind the third base line, his eyes fixed on the batter's box, was their head coach, the only one in purple who had been this close to Omaha before. Closer, actually. Nine years earlier, as a twenty-six-year-old head coach at Western Carolina, his team had been just two outs from defeating Florida State and blazing an improbable trail to the CWS. Since his arrival at ECU in 1997, Keith LeClair had been imprinting a new mental template in these Pirates. Omaha is not only a real and tangible goal, he told them, it's the only goal for a college baseball player. And, even for a school that had never won an NCAA regional before its new coach arrived in 1997, Omaha was possible.

A hammering downpour soaked Grainger Stadium in Kinston on the Friday night before the first game, putting the schedule in doubt before the Super Regional even got underway. But the field dried out sufficiently, and a raucous ECU crowd made the short drive down NC-11 to be witnesses, they hoped, to history. The Pirates' roster featured a loaded senior class including Cliff Godwin and Joseph Hastings, who later became Division I coaches, and Chad Tracy, who went on to a solid major-league career with the Arizona Diamondbacks. Pitching for the Volunteers was Wyatt Allen, who would soon be selected in the first round of the Major League Baseball Amateur Draft.

Allen, the recently-named MVP of the NCAA Regional in Knoxville, hadn't slowed that momentum on the trip to Kinston. In his first six innings, he so silenced the Pirate bats that Tennessee had constructed a 9–2 lead. But then the East Carolina hitters heated up—Chad Tracy led the charge with a three-run home run in the eighth—and by the advent of the ninth inning the Pirates had surged to a 10–9 lead.

The most conflicted person on the field that day had to be Tennessee assistant coach Randy Mazey, who had served as an East Carolina assistant the season before and had recruited many of the players on both teams. He was also an old friend of LeClair's, and he knew that his friend had lost weight and had complained of some unusual symptoms in recent months. As he watched Keith across the field, he felt that the outcome of this tournament could be more enduring than most.

"The thing that I can see, like it was yesterday, was when Tennessee was up 9–7 in the eighth inning, and then Chad Tracy hit a three-run homer to take the lead. I looked at Keith, who was coaching third base, and he pumped his fist, got excited, and jumped up and down. Even though that home run took away the lead of the team I was coaching for,

LeClair congratulates Chad Tracy on his way around the bases in a 2001 NCAA Regional game against Winthrop in Wilson, N.C. Tracy went on to a successful major league career with the Arizona Diamondbacks.

I was really, really happy for Keith at that time."

With hope in their throats, LeClair's team took the field for the ninth, needing only to hold the visiting Vols and then defeat them the next day to book their Omaha flights. But Tennessee assembled a classic ninth-inning rally for a 13–10 win in a game several UT players called the best they had ever been a part of.

In the second game, ECU came out fighting again, leading 3–1 into the eighth inning. But Tennessee's Stevie Daniels made his imprint in the eighth with a grand slam home run that erased ECU's edge and led to a 6–3 win. That second Volunteer surge in as many days shut the door firmly on the most tantalizing College World Series hopes the Pirate Nation had ever tasted.

Of the sixteen regional tournaments and eleven Super Regional games that had been played to that point in 2001, around 85 percent had gone to the home team. So that made ECU part of a heartbreaking minority, with a short trip back to Greenville ahead and a thrill-packed season over. It was no surprise that grown men—and elite athletes at that—were crying as the team gathered near the right field fence for LeClair's final postgame words.

"The thing I will always remember and carry with me everywhere from here on out is what Coach LeClair told us after that playoff game," said Joe Hastings, one of the top hitters on that ECU team.

They sat in the outfield, an assembly of dashed hopes, and turned their attention to their coach. Just thirty-five years old and already a decade into his collegiate head coaching career, LeClair was still so strong that he could outlift any of them in the weight room. He was a man so driven he had once broken his wrist chasing a loose ball at a high school basketball scrimmage. As a player at Western Carolina University, he would beg his teammates to stay at the batting cages to pitch to him late into the night. He had always taken losses so hard that he avoided seeing anyone afterwards, choosing instead to steal away and dissect the elements of the game that had gone wrong. He had single-handedly made the word "Omaha" the heartbeat of the Pirate baseball program. If anyone had reason to feel disconsolate as Tennessee celebrated across the diamond, it was the man they called simply "Coach."

He was visibly distraught as he reminded the players of how many hurdles they had cleared during the season. He said a word to honor the team's seniors, told them all he was proud of them, said all of the things that a coach who put his players first should say. But then he said something that seemed to freeze in the air, a statement that under other circumstances might have been remembered as mere inspiration. He told his team, "If this is the worst thing that ever happens to you, then you will have lived a successful life."

As the players ambled away lead-footed to collect their

things and board the bus, LeClair spotted ECU athletic director Mike Hamrick across the field and walked to meet him behind second base. Hamrick, who calls LeClair the best hiring decision he has made in twenty years, was prepared to encourage the coach who had already taken his school's baseball program to unprecedented heights. Instead, LeClair spoke first, and with so much emotion that Hamrick was taken aback.

"I've let you down," LeClair said to Hamrick through tears. Everyone associated with ECU was devastated in those minutes, but Hamrick never thought to condemn his baseball coach for a season that had thrust ECU into the national spotlight.

Both encounters—the coach addressing his players and his boss—would have faded into the hearers' memories if life had continued in its normal rhythms—another offseason, fall conditioning, the hopeful dawn of a new schedule, more postseason opportunities, the whole thing ending and then starting all over again. But to those who loved Coach LeClair, everything about that weekend would later seem like it was written in bold type. His New Hampshire cadence as he answered questions from the media seemed a bit unsteady—they realized when they listened months later—even from a New Englander in the Deep South. They would recall how tired he was in the weeks before the regional, how much weight he was losing, how he seemed to get worn out from throwing batting practice.

And to a man, they said the same thing: "I think he knew."

It would be weeks before LeClair would have a name for the disease, and months before he would painstakingly rule out any other possibility. But he approached that postgame with a grim finality, and with the emotion of a man whose laser focus would soon be directed at a much more formidable opponent.

"I believe Keith knew," Hamrick said. "I don't think he'd officially been told. But I think he knew he was sick, and he knew that was his last chance to go to Omaha. And that was his whole dream."

Four years later, in a letter to assistant coach George Whitfield, LeClair would reflect on that moment and conclude that, as unclear as the future was, the words he spoke to his team that day originated from a God who was in control.

"Thinking back on it, I believe God was speaking to me when I told the guys that if this is the worst thing that ever happens to you, you will have had a great life," he wrote in January 2003. "Those were the last words I ever spoke in uniform. Oh, how quickly things change in the blink of an eye. All we truly have in life are our memories with our closest friends and what we do for others."

2

Walpole

IF A HOLLYWOOD PRODUCER WAS TO ASK A SET DIRECTOR for a locale called "Typical New England Village," the result would bear an uncanny resemblance to Walpole, New Hampshire. This town of 3,500, founded in 1752, formed the picturesque backdrop for the man and coach Keith LeClair would become. He lived with older sisters Sharon and Sharlene, older brother Kevin, and parents Andy and Doris in a wood frame house situated on a hilly lot outside of Walpole.

Walpole is the type of place that evokes Norman Rockwell paintings, with destinations in the heart of town like the Village Green, the Village Tavern and adjoining Village Market, and a classic white, clapboard town hall. LeClair attended the Walpole School for grades kindergarten through eighth, and the school and nearby recreational leagues supplied a succession of sports teams that honed his skills at baseball, basketball, and football.

Keith's brother Kevin remembers a happy childhood, full of practical joking and athletic competition, even if his family had its share of struggles. As kids, Keith and his friends played baseball or basketball past sunset, often braving the bitter New England cold to finish out an impromptu game. Brian Pickering was a year older than Keith, and they started playing Little League together when they were only eight or nine. For the next ten years, they were part of a group of boys who pushed each other every time they stepped onto a baseball diamond or a basketball hardwood. When they weren't

*Keith, age 5, outside his
family's home in Walpole.*

playing sports, they were replaying a past game or planning
for the next one. "Keith was sleeping and talking about baseball," said childhood friend Dean Gay.

"It was after school, it was the conversations during school,
it was summer," said Pickering, now a high school principal
in Swanzey, New Hampshire, about twenty-five miles from
Walpole. "It was just constant. It's what drove us."

There were times when Kevin saw his younger brother
Keith as a pest, especially when he tagged along and got in
the way of the older boys' activities. But then, on many a lazy
New Hampshire afternoon, the two would set up their hilly
backyard for a Wiffleball game, and brothers became fierce
competitors.

The intricate rules for the LeClair Brothers Wiffleball
League prove that this was no casual backyard pastime. It
was one-on-one ball, except for the part played by the metal
lawn chairs that marked the bases. If the pitcher threw the
ball to the chair and it hit its target before the runner reached
the base, the runner was out. If the ball bounced once and
landed into the tall grass in center field, that was a ground
rule double. A ball hit over the three apple trees and into the

Little Leaguer, age 8.

tall grass was a home run. Over the chicken shed in right field was also a home run, but Kevin always told his left-handed brother that he had an advantage, because the chicken shed gave him an easy home run in right.

"We'd make up all of these rules as we went along," said Kevin, who lives with his family in the same house where he and Keith grew up and played those Wiffleball games. "He came up with all of these things, like, 'It's a triple off the chicken shed,' and I would say, 'How do you get a triple off the chicken shed?' And he would say, 'Because it's a real small object. It's hard to hit.'"

Even as they tried to outdo each other with the swing of a plastic bat, Kevin noticed that his kid brother's athletic prowess was drawing attention beyond the LeClair backyard field. He and some of his friends would frequently go play a modified game of basketball at a building they had converted and named the Little Hoops Association (LHA). One afternoon when Kevin was a senior in high school and Keith was in the eighth grade, the older boys were getting a group together to go play at LHA and one of his friends said, "Hey, why don't you bring Keith?"

"Keith?" Kevin responded. "Why?"

"He's pretty good," his friend said, forcing Kevin to rethink his opinion of Keith as a pesky kid brother.

Embedded in those no-holds-barred Wiffleball games and Little Hoops contests were the seeds of an aim that would set the trajectory of Keith's life. Even as a kid, he was characterized by competitive intensity and a single track goal—to so excel in the sport of baseball that he would one day play in the major leagues. Friends and family from Walpole described him, variously, as "[having] the drive to be the best he can be," "very goal-oriented," "as focused a kid as I've ever seen," and "someone who really knew what he wanted to do."

John Chandler coached Keith in Little League baseball for three years. What Chandler remembers most about young Keith was his eagerness to learn the fundamentals of the game—to master the fine points of bunting or base running. "Whenever you would teach something new, his ears would perk right up," he said. John had taken on the post to help his younger brother Brian, one of Keith's close friends. But when Brian aged out of Little League and Keith still had one year, John stayed on as the coach, he said, just because of Keith.

The Campbell family lived across the street from the LeClairs for decades, and at a young age Keith became a fixture at the Campbell home. Jeff Campbell, the youngest of three boys, was like a brother to Keith, and Jeff's mom Pat Campbell remembers one day when Keith had been at her house for three days and the telephone rang. "(Keith's father) Andy called, and said, 'Is that LeClair kid over there? Would you tell him his mother and dad would like to see him?'" Pat Campbell recalled.

Behind the Campbells' house sat a backyard pool and a screened pool house, and there were summers when Jeff and Keith made a change of address to that screen house. They swam every waking moment, Pat Campbell said, with an occasional break for baseball. On the other seasonal extreme, she remembers an extreme New Hampshire blizzard that knocked the power out. The Campbells had a fireplace, and the LeClairs didn't. "They all came over and stayed a couple of days," she said. "We wrapped pots and pans in foil and cooked in the fireplace, and the kids all slept in sleeping bags in the floor."

When Joe Milliken moved to nearby North Walpole as a seventh grader, Keith was one of the first classmates he met, and he said that his new friend stood out from the other preteens, not just because he was a natural athlete, but because of his demeanor that often made him seem older than his years. "He was down to earth, very quiet but not introverted," Milliken said. "It just seemed like he was focused."

After finishing eighth grade at Walpole School, Keith enrolled at Fall Mountain Regional High School, a school of around 700 students that served the New Hampshire towns of Walpole, North Walpole, Alstead, Langdon, and Charlestown. He arrived on campus hoping to play for the Wildcats in all three major sports, and as a freshman he pulled that off. But he soon realized that the demands of football and basketball might interfere too much with his baseball dreams. So his football career ended there, and he didn't go out for the basketball team as a sophomore, telling Coach Kevin Haverty that he wanted to attend the Denny Doyle Baseball Camp in Winter Haven, Florida, in February and that commitment would conflict with the end of the basketball season.

With a professional baseball career in his sights, Keith doggedly sought out the appropriate steps toward that destination and took them. Coaches told him that he needed to bulk up, so he was a constant presence in the weight room. And when he read an advertisement touting the Denny Doyle Camp as the ideal way for a young player to improve his skills, he signed up and flew to Florida alone. He was only fifteen.

During that first week at the Doyle camp, LeClair was

named Camper of the Week and invited to return for two weeks the following winter. So as his junior year dawned, Keith was already committed to another Florida trip. But he came to realize something else: Even if it wasn't his first love, he really missed basketball. His friends remembered him as a gifted shooter with a sublime baseline jumper who could excel as both a shooting guard and a small forward. Kevin Haverty, Keith's former head coach, observed him as a freshman and knew he was a coach's dream, so it pained him when Keith passed on the sport as a sophomore. Haverty vividly remembered the conversation he had with Keith during the fall of 1982, when Keith was a junior.

"He missed it," Haverty said of basketball. "One or two weeks into the season he came in and said, 'Coach, I would like to play.'"

"Great, what about baseball camp?" Haverty said.

"That's what I want to talk about," Keith told him. "I still want to go to that. I really miss basketball, and I love it, but my goal is to be a baseball player."

Haverty decided to bring it to the other members of the team. He gathered them around and told them that Keith wanted to join, but the Doyle baseball camp would mean that he would miss the basketball playoffs. And even though Keith would be starting the season late and leaving it early, every player in that locker room said that they wanted him to be their teammate. "I loved Keith so much," Haverty said. "He was such a great influence on the other kids and just a wonderful person. And they all felt the same way about him. Sure enough, he played, and he played great. He was just heart and soul, really."

Not long after the Fall Mountain Regional team voted Keith into their ranks, Haverty broke up an intense practice with one of the players' favorite drills: the Wild Man scrimmage. In the Wild Man, fouls weren't called and rebounds and steals were awarded points as well as baskets. It was a drill that rewarded tenacity, and no one was more tenacious in an everyday practice than Keith.

That afternoon, he was battling for a loose ball with close friend Dean Gay. While both boys knocked into each other to grab the precious ball, they scuffled right into the wall of the gym. The momentum caused Dean to push Keith into the wall, and the force broke Keith's wrist. "What I remember is him going into the wall full speed ahead," said teammate Brian Pickering.

The doctor put Keith's left hand—his shooting hand—in a cast, but he showed up at every practice, dribbling diligently with his right hand. In the end, the injury may have made him a better player, Haverty said, because he was forced to become more ambidextrous. That accident was indicative of Keith's general attitude every time he stepped onto a court or field—all out, all the time. He might have opted to miss some key basketball games because of his baseball goals, but he was unwilling to sacrifice one ounce of effort when he was out there, even if his full-bore basketball style put his body at risk.

Coaches like Haverty tend to be idealistic realists: They have an image of how the quintessential team player would execute plays, and they urge their athletes to perform that way. But those players are teenagers, and most of them stop short of pushing themselves beyond logical limits. But Keith was that rare player who absorbed a coach's advice and then turned around and heeded it. Imagine a situation where a team is pressing on defense, but the player with the ball beats the press and goes tearing down the floor to take a shot, Haverty said. Many defenders would just jog a few steps and then accept the inevitable basket. "Keith would come barreling out of nowhere, and he'd dive from eight feet behind the guy, slide across the floor and knock the ball out, and then get up. We'd get the ball and he'd be on the other end scoring a layup. And he'd not only do that in games. He'd do it in practice as well. There was no such thing as shielding his body from getting hurt. He wanted to be the best."

After the Christmas break, Keith's wrist was strong and he was back in full force, and he helped spark the Wildcats to the New Hampshire state playoffs. But just as the playoffs started, exactly as he said he would, he left for baseball camp in Florida.

The Wildcats lost in double overtime in those playoffs, Haverty said, overachieving against a higher-seeded team. The coach is sure, as he looks back over twenty-five years, that they would have won that year with Keith, but he isn't the least bit surprised that the young man with that natural jumper followed through on his commitment to pour himself into baseball. That decision was completely consistent with every other part of Keith's life to that point, he said.

"He's one of the first kids I've ever known that had that dream, but they didn't just screw around and play pick-up and summer league," Haverty said. "He did all the things he was supposed to do. He was in the weight room every day. The thing I admired was that he wanted to have both, and I understood that, but he didn't have to tell me that he was going to leave. I was just praying that he would change his mind."

Pickering was a senior on that team, and it represented his last shot at a state basketball title. He wasn't angry about Keith's decision, but he didn't really understand it. From his teenage perspective, flying off to Florida during the basketball playoffs wasn't logical. Also at that point, if someone had told him that Keith would excel as a baseball player at a Division I university, he would have been doubtful, because Keith didn't necessarily stand out as more athletic than any other starter at Fall Mountain High. What he didn't grasp then, but understood with clarity as an adult, was that Keith was undergirded by extraordinary determination and a laser focus. "I think the difference between him and most of us is that he really knew what he wanted to do from a very early age, and we didn't," Pickering said.

"At the time we all thought we were good, but I think we also knew that he was a little more dedicated," childhood friend Dean Gay said of Keith and baseball. "I don't think we knew his desire. We all think we had the same desire, but when it comes right down to it, we didn't."

Each March, when the calendar said that winter was coming to a close but New Hampshire hadn't received the memo, LeClair would suit up for baseball under the watchful eye of Hank Beecher, who was still coaching at Fall Mountain Regional in 2009 after more than thirty-five years in that post. Beecher coached close to a thousand young men in those years, either at the high school or in American Legion baseball, but Keith belongs to a tiny select group of those athletes who played with unyielding enthusiasm, worked harder than they had to, and loved every intricacy of the game of baseball.

"On bus trips, he would sit near the front, and he'd be asking questions, talking very technical terms about pitch sequence, and 'Should I have done something different?'" Beecher said. "A lot of kids would just say, 'Are we going to McDonald's?' But Keith would be thinking about the game. And that's a rarity. Even as a freshman, he wanted to know how things worked. It was really refreshing to see. I take it serious. I'm very intense. And he was the same way."

Beecher saw many players with more raw talent than LeClair come through the program, young men with better arms, more speed, and a stronger swing. But Keith, who pitched and played first base for the Wildcats, was resolute and driven and unlikely to make the same mistake twice. He was confident and capable enough to make smooth transitions along the way—from the freshman team to the varsity, from Walpole American Legion to the larger Senior Babe Ruth in Keene, from high school to college. Over the years, ime to believe the secret to a player's success lay in ability to make those adjustments. "He was always able to turn it up a notch when he needed to," Beecher said. "That's the mark of a good baseball player."

In the early to mid-1980s, Walpole and its surrounding towns were known for producing exceptional baseball players, and the sport had a considerable following in those towns. That passion for the sport fueled local rivalries, and no rivalry created more excitement than the one between the Babe Ruth teams from Walpole and nearby North Walpole. Keith and his friends competed in Babe Ruth between the ages of thirteen and fifteen, and Joe Milliken said that Keith's Walpole squad perennially had the upper hand.

"Half of the boys in the class at school played for one, and half played for the other," said Milliken, who was on the North Walpole team. "For as small a town as Walpole is, they had so many awesome baseball players. And we had a few on our team too, but we could never beat Walpole. They were so good."

Sometime in his teens, by the time he joined the varsity at Fall Mountain Regional, Keith had decided that his jersey number of choice was 23. Kevin LeClair remembers that his brother chose that number in homage to Don Mattingly, the legendary Yankees hitter who also wore 23. Milliken, who later became a sportswriter for a weekly newspaper covering the Walpole area, always thought that LeClair and Mattingly had more in common than just the digits on their jerseys. "He reminded me of Don Mattingly," Milliken said. "He was skinny, but strong. A left-handed batter and thrower. He played first base. He could hit for average and power. And they both wore 23."

The number 23 would be significant for the rest of Keith's life, and it endures still for those closest to him. Because baseball is the only sport where coaches wear uniforms with numbers, he was able to keep his number through most of his playing career and, except for a few years at the beginning, for all of his coaching years.

If Keith was atypical in his diligence as a student of baseball, he also went against the grain by defying most "typical teenager" stereotypes. Part of his single-track approach to achieving his baseball dreams meant that drinking, drugs, and girls were unwanted distractions for him. "Sometimes high school kids will experiment with drugs or alcohol or something like that, but that just wasn't Keith," Kevin said. "He loved to have fun, but he knew the difference between right and wrong."

Joe Milliken and Dean Gay, two of his closest friends in high school, remember only one time they convinced Keith to drink a beer—and it wasn't at a wild party but on a night when the three boys were hanging out at Dean's house after a spirited basketball game. They kept playing, pushing each other and talking trash, even when raindrops turned into big, wet flakes of snow. For Gay, it was one of those nights of childhood that seems suspended in the silken strands of memory, those flashes where the details are uncommonly vivid. It was March 5, 1982, the night of comedian John Belushi's death, and Rick Robey had just helped their favorite NBA team, the Celtics, defeat the Sixers on a last-second tip-in. After playing basketball for hours, the three toasted Belushi with a beer. "It was one of those magical nights," Gay recalled.

Even Keith's teenage fun was tempered with baseball discipline, his friends said. Gay remembers trying to convince Keith to attend a school dance, which commenced a negotiation. "He'd say, 'OK, if I do 100 pushups, we'll go to the dance.' 'And I think I said, OK, I'll do it with you.' And I would do twenty, and then he would do two hundred to make up for me." His reading material of choice, during free time, was almost always instructional baseball books, and he would come to practice armed with new hitting tips from experts

*Senior year (1984)
at Fall Mountain
Regional High School.*

like Rod Carew and Tony Gwynn. And in the summers, especially in college when Keith and many of his friends were playing college baseball, it was always Keith urging his friends to lift more, to complete their summer workouts before taking time for diversions.

For a baseball player in Walpole, early summer high school baseball playoffs would transition seamlessly into Babe Ruth or American Legion ball. Keith had been part of the Legion team that was also coached by Beecher for three summers, but for the summer before his senior year in high school he changed tracks and chose to drive to Keene—about twenty minutes away—to play on the Senior Babe Ruth team there.

The Legion team had a new coach that Keith was unsure about, Kevin said, but a larger consideration was Keith's feeling that he would get noticed by more college recruiters playing Senior Babe Ruth, a league that involved travel to big tournaments. College baseball was the next rung on the ladder, and Keith wanted to do everything possible to put himself on an NCAA Division I roster. He also welcomed the opportunity to play for John Waterston, the coach of the Keene SBR team and a local baseball legend.

Before that summer, Keith had already had a few conversations with Western Carolina head coach Jack Leggett, who had recruited Keith's friend Brian Chandler the previous year before Chandler committed to the University of North Carolina. Beecher had also contacted Leggett on Keith's behalf. Beecher had recommended that Leggett consider Keith and his Fall Mountain Regional teammate Tim Hennessey, and from one coach to another, he told Leggett that he thought Keith had more potential for college success than an observer might initially see. "I said, 'I've got this kid, and what he lacks in ability, he makes up for. He's like another coach on the field,'" Beecher said.

After that exchange, Keith flew down to Cullowhee, North Carolina, on his own to investigate. He liked the campus and made a quick connection with Leggett, a blue-collar coach with New England roots. Leggett has a memory of this young, eager recruit, wearing a "Boston Red Sox" painter's cap, soaking up every aspect of the campus and the baseball program.

Keith was still undecided about his collegiate path that summer when, traveling with the Keene team, he had an unforgettable stretch of games in a tournament in Massachusetts that was well attended by college coaches. Other coaches expressed an interest at that tournament, but LeClair had enjoyed his visit to Western Carolina and felt drawn there, even if Leggett couldn't offer him any scholarship money. "He was very impressionable, and the next thing I knew after his visit, he went back home and decided to come here," Leggett said.

In New Hampshire, high school baseball practice starts around March 20. In North Carolina, the preseason opens on February 1. That disparity alone explains Keith's number one criteria in choosing a college—warm weather. He had spent mere weeks in Florida, but it was enough to show him that he couldn't follow his baseball life plan in an area that only allows about four months of the sport a year. So he had set his sights on the South, but the Vermont-born Leggett offered him a slice of home, too. Western seemed like the right fit.

His teammate Hennessey was reluctant to travel that far from home, and he wasn't as determined as Keith to leave the North. When Leggett offered both young men opportunities to come to WCU, Hennessey signed too, but he knew right away that Keith was taking it more seriously than he was. "I thought he was right in his element," he said. "He fit right in there." For most of the next thirteen years Keith would stay in that little mountain town, over time discovering the seeds of his future family, his faith, and the career that hadn't even occurred to him when he was an eighteen-year-old with the big leagues in his sights.

3
Cullowhee

CULLOWHEE WAS 1,000 MILES FROM WALPOLE, BUT THERE was plenty in the small Appalachian hamlet that recalled LeClair's home. Both towns were scenic and green, with roads that snake through the hills. Both offered only a couple of restaurants and the probability that you would run into someone you knew at every turn. And, the common thread that had carried LeClair to these unfamiliar environs: Both took their baseball seriously.

Keith came to Western with Tim Hennessey, but Hennessey was homesick and ill at ease in Cullowhee and returned to Walpole after the fall semester. That left Keith, fixed on this university of 8,000 as the place that would allow him to fulfill his baseball dreams. But observers both back home and at his new school wondered if he would make it much longer than his friend.

"I always said that a thousand miles was a lot farther distance than what he thought when he went there," said his mother. "We let him come home at Thanksgiving, because he really wanted to come home. And then when he went back, he was fine. He wasn't homesick anymore."

As Keith settled into dorm life and classes, the baseball coaching staff was trying to assess what kind of raw material their new walk-on brought to the team. He was bowlegged, head coach Jack Leggett said, with an unceasing work ethic and, to use standard coachspeak, "a lot of potential." Graduate assistant coach Bill Currier said he was subpar in both speed and strength, but his hitting skills stood out. Even though his friends and coaches in Walpole considered him exceptionally fit, the NCAA Division I standard demanded much more of its athletes.

"That first year Jack told him, 'You need to work out more. You need to get stronger," said Steve White, a longtime WCU athletic administrator who was the sports information director during Keith's years there. "I really didn't think he would come back his second year. Because his first year he was not an impact player."

As a freshman, Keith played in thirty-five games and had twenty-two hits. But he was single-minded about improving and becoming more of a factor on the squad that finished 37–35 and won the Southern Conference that year. Keith Shumate, who arrived in Cullowhee at the same time as LeClair, remembers hoping for his teammate's success as much as his own. "He wanted to prove himself, and he wanted that respect, and he wasn't sure at the very beginning that everybody believed in him," Shumate said. "We'd be the first guys to go hit every single day."

Currier was charged with helping the young players improve their strength and speed. As a winter workout technique toward that end, he took Keith LeClair and Keith Shumate to WCU's indoor pool on frigid days. "I had them running in the pool all winter, and Keith [LeClair] thought I was trying to kill him," Currier said. "He really wasn't crazy about the water."

When his sophomore season dawned, everyone who laid eyes on Keith realized that he had heeded his head coach's advice and hit the weight room. Just five feet eleven and 178 pounds when he came in as a freshman, Keith had gained fourteen pounds of muscle when he started his sophomore season. His physique was so changed that Currier gave him a new nickname that stuck for the duration of his years at Western, dubbing him "Condo." "He was really into the lifting," Currier explained. "He knew that to become a better hitter, stronger was the key. After his freshman year, I told him, 'You're not quite as big as a house, but you're kind of a condo.'"

More strength translated into more power during Keith's sophomore season, when he collected forty hits in fifty-five games, including one home run and twenty-six RBI. He also developed a reputation as the player who could make others look bad with his unflagging work ethic, the one who would drag pitcher friends away from evening plans so that they could throw to him after hours in the batting cages. Steve White remembers seeing one light on in the batting cages when he would pass by at night, and it was nearly always Le-Clair swinging away, trying to get an edge on any pitcher he would face in future contests.

Clint Fairey, who joined the WCU team when Keith was a sophomore, remembers the hard work too, but he was also struck by how soft-spoken and laid-back Keith was, despite his intensity. Keith was one of a dozen New England players that Jack had recruited during those years, and Fairey—a South Carolina native—wasn't sure what to make of so many Northerners. But Keith seemed to belie his Southern stereotypes. "He was way too laid back to be a Yankee," Fairey said.

After his friend Hennessey headed back North, Keith didn't have peers around him who knew of his straight-laced high school image, so he could have easily let loose a little in college without anyone thinking it unusual. But a wild streak was just incompatible with LeClair's single-track, goal-oriented character, so his college friends had to probe their memories for even a single rebellious act. "He never wanted to get in trouble," Fairey said.

But Fairey does remember one incident, when WCU had just constructed an ice skating rink on campus. LeClair and some of his "Yankee" friends, who grew up following hockey, had the idea to commandeer that ice for an impromptu hockey game. They found a way in without permission and recruited their teammates for a rowdy hockey face-off with brooms and tennis balls, wearing tennis shoes on the ice. As head coaches tend to do, Leggett found out about their icy adventure, and they paid for it in practice the next day. "Leggett ran us," Fairey said. "I remember my tongue was dragging the ground. That was the only thing I remember that he did that wasn't what he was supposed to do."

LeClair's upward progression continued during the 1987 season, his junior year. He batted .372 with eighty-four hits, nine home runs and eighty-four RBI. He was starting to exceed some observers' expectations of him, despite limited physical advantages, because he was determined to outwork the natural athletes and get there the hard way. "He was an extremely hard worker, blue collar; he was right up my alley," Leggett said. "He loved to play; he was a student of the game. He was always trying to learn more about it."

Leggett does remember one time, later in his college career, when Keith's determination seemed tepid. Leggett, known as a pure player's coach and an adept motivator, called his first baseman into the dugout for a one-on-one. "I remember telling him, 'You're not playing like Keith LeClair plays, you're being tentative, you're not being aggressive, you're not being quite as coachable. What's going on?'" Leggett said. "And I remember the look in his eyes. It was painful to him that he had let me down. I could see tears come in his eyes, and he said, 'I can't believe that you're having to tell me this.' Right after that, he started to play, and he started to realize what his roots were."

Like most college baseball players, LeClair looked to summer leagues as an opportunity to improve his skills and play as much ball as possible. Fairey particularly recalled one summer when he and Keith played together in the Valley Baseball League in Virginia. Their team, the Staunton Braves, won the championship that summer, and they maintained a busy schedule. Even though they stayed with a local family, the league didn't pay them a salary, and the team owner had to help them find jobs to support their baseball habit. They started out working in an auto parts warehouse, Fairey said, but then they went through lifeguard training and starting working at the pool at Shenandoah Acres Resort. It was an ideal combination, according to Fairey: "Lifeguards during the day, and ballplayers at night."

But the true culmination of Keith's perseverance came during his senior year, when he had one of the most productive seasons of any hitter in Western Carolina history. He batted .423 with 101 hits, eighteen home runs and sixty-seven RBI. Everything seemed to click during his last season, and his coaches knew that his confidence was at its zenith. He memorably batted .600 and hit twelve RBI in the Southern Conference Tournament, which his team won for the fourth consecutive year, and he was named MVP of the event. That charmed season lives on in the Catamount record books, as LeClair still holds the record for hits in a season and stands at second in total bases in a season and seventh in single-season batting average.

"What he transformed himself into his senior year was one of the best hitters that I recall seeing on our team or on any other team that we faced that season," said Tim Sinicki, a friend and teammate of Keith's that year. "He was just locked in."

Even one of Keith's greatest advocates—his old New Hampshire high school coach—was taken aback by the reports that reached him from the Appalachian mountains. "It kind of amazed me a bit," Hank Beecher said. "I knew he would do well, but I never thought he would do that well. He accomplished more than he probably should have. He exceeded, probably, his own expectations."

As an upperclassmen, LeClair was a quiet leader, showing younger players the way mostly by example, his teammates say. But Shumate recalls one time when his friend's convictions about what was right nearly led to a fight in the dugout. A freshman player came in wearing an earring, Shumate said, and while wearing earrings wasn't expressly forbidden, LeClair felt that it went against the standards that WCU athletes were supposed to represent. LeClair asked the player to remove his earring, and when he refused Keith got angry and threatened the younger teammate physically. Shumate had to separate the two and help make peace.

While Keith was toiling away at Western's Childress Field and trying to keep younger teammates focused, the central figure in another Catamount sport was involved in the fight of his life. Bob Waters, the head football coach at WCU for two decades, was battling ALS (amyotrophic lateral sclerosis). Waters' deterioration gripped the close-knit campus and left the Catamount community heartbroken when he died in 1989 at the age of fifty. When Keith left WCU in 1997 to take the head coaching job at East Carolina, he would bring a framed picture of Waters from his office in Cullowhee to his new office across the state. Friends wondered why he felt compelled to pack the picture, especially years later when the two coaches became linked by much more than Western Carolina.

Keith left Western in 1988, still a few credits shy of his degree, to take on the next logical step for a baseball player with his hopes pinned on the major leagues. He signed with the Atlanta Braves farm organization and was sent to the Idaho Falls Braves, a rookie-level club in the Pioneer League. During that 1988 season, he batted .264 and had fifty-five hits, but he didn't stand out on the roster, and his brother Kevin said he was disillusioned by the minor league culture. It was a jarring descent—from the heights of such an unforgettable senior year to a lonely Idaho outpost with a 28–42 record.

When Keith's brother and his mom had a minute to talk to him between bus rides and countless hotel stays, they sensed that he was starting to rethink that big-league dream. "I don't think the experience was what he thought it was," Kevin Le-Clair said. "I remember him calling me and telling me that a kid who was the best ballplayer on the whole team was so sick of the minor leagues that he just quit. Keith tried it, but he was just disillusioned by the whole process." And Doris LeClair added: "I think he thought there was a lot of politics to it."

He was released after one season in Idaho Falls and was invited to attend spring training with the San Francisco Giants organization, and that camp was his last reach for the bigs. His play at that spring camp wasn't stellar enough to open any more doors, and in the spring of 1989 he hung up his cleats and the major-league dream that had steered him since childhood and returned to the North Carolina mountain town that had become a second home.

In twenty-nine years of coaching, Jack Leggett's teams have produced more than thirty Division I college coaches, and at least one former player said that he gave such a thorough baseball education that anyone could coach after four years under his tutelage. But in truth, Leggett said, only one or two players a year really have the goods to excel in coaching, and Keith hadn't been wearing a Catamount uniform long before Leggett had pegged him as one of those.

"There are a lot that understand the game, that like the game, but to have the passion, the patience, the communication skills, the fundamental awareness, the work ethic and the motivation, you have to have all of those things in line," Leggett said. "It was easy to see early on that he was going to be a really good coach. He had that ability to teach and communicate, to relate to the players. He just had that light in his eyes and that enthusiasm that was infectious."

Leggett offered Keith a job as a Catamount assistant coach while he finished his degree. He jumped at the chance even though he started his new career as a volunteer and then progressed to a salary of $14,000 a year. Paul Menhart was a freshman when LeClair was a power-hitting senior, and Le-Clair's strength and leadership made an impression on him then. When Menhart was a junior—his last collegiate season before signing with the Toronto Blue Jays—LeClair became his team's assistant coach, and Menhart discovered that he had more to learn from his ex-teammate.

"I came in as a really cocky freshman, and to watch him play the game the way it was supposed to be played, it was so influential to me," Menhart said. "He taught me those things that go beyond baseball—work ethic and responsibility."

It was after his return to Western that Keith met Lynn Winchester, a young lady from Shady Grove, South Carolina, just over the mountain from Cullowhee. Lynn's sister Christle was a student at WCU, and she was dating one of Keith's friends. Lynn came up to visit and met Keith, and before long Keith was stopping by the Winchester home when he was out on recruiting trips. As he and Lynn began dating, he also became very close to her family. Keith would stop by with coaching friends and ask Lynn's mother Donna to cook Southern dishes for them, and he formed an immediate bond with her father, Doug. Because they all got along so well and Keith's budget was so tight, dates usually consisted of dinner with her parents.

But after they had been dating seriously for a while, Keith came over the mountain one night and told Lynn he wanted to take her out alone. They went to a restaurant at Table Rock State Park, and after dinner drove to nearby Lake Keowee. Keith was nervous that Lynn might drop the ring in the lake. They were married on June 22, 1991, in a small South Carolina mountain chapel called Pretty Place.

Lynn moved to Cullowhee, fresh out of college, and got her first elementary school teaching job while Keith prepared for his second year as an assistant coach. But head coach Leggett was hearing his own kind of proposal from a place over the mountain: Clemson University, just thirty-five miles from Lynn's home town. Clemson, a Division I baseball powerhouse, wanted to hire Leggett as an assistant coach with the promise that he would succeed long-time head coach Bill Wilhelm after two years.

Leggett was torn about the Clemson offer. He loved Western and was protective of the legacy he had helped build there, but he knew that a chance like this might not come along again. He resolved to accept the job, but he was equally committed to influencing the WCU athletic officials to replace him with the kind of coach who would continue to coach according to his ideals. He was sure that the perfect new head coach had been right there in front of them for years, even if he was only twenty-five years old.

"I felt like if I could leave the program in really good hands, it would be a little easier for me to leave," Leggett said. "There was a period there where they were uncertain whether they were going to offer the job to Keith or whether they were going to open the job up. I was very distraught. He was young, but the foundation of the program had been set, and he had been a big part of it. It was really important to me to see someone who had been in the program take over the program, someone who knew what the expectation level was."

The respect level for Leggett was so high on the WCU campus that they agreed to give LeClair a chance, even though the local newspaper at the time emblazoned a picture of the inexperienced new coach with the heading, "Big Shoes to Fill." Keith took the reins in 1992, leading the team he had played first base for only four years earlier. He was believed to be the youngest Division I head coach in the nation at that time.

"When Jack left, he jokingly said, 'He'll probably go to the NCAA Regionals next year. He'll probably go to Omaha. He knows more about it than I do,'" recalled Steve White. The early games in Keith's first season as head coach were rocky.

*Coach LeClair, just 25 years old when he took the reins
at Western Carolina, motivates his team before a 1992
NCAA Regional game during his first season as the WCU
head coach.*

Bill Jarman, Keith's assistant coach, was himself only twenty-
seven, and he and Keith laid out about eighteen rules for the
players in an effort to assert authority. "Some of the seniors
played with him, and they were still calling him Keith," Jarman said. "We had to change that." As time went on, Jarman
said, they backed off on the excessive rules and won the players' trust through commitment and strong communication.

The Catamounts lost seven out of their first eight games
that year, but they found their stride, and they ended up with
a 44–21–1 record and an invitation to the NCAA Regional in
Tallahassee. The first part of Leggett's prediction had come
true, and baseball fans in Cullowhee still cringe when they
remember how close they were to tasting the second part—
Omaha.

LeClair had just turned twenty-six, and his unknown Catamounts came to Florida and promptly shut out the first two
seeds—Florida State 1–0 on the first day, and Stanford 5–0 on

the second. The regional was heady stuff for a young coach from the mountains, and he worried about how he would sound talking to the throng of reporters who were casting his team as the ultimate underdog. But when LeClair and Jarman got back to the hotel after the Stanford victory, they finally had a chance to act their age and show their jubilation. "We were so young and excited, but still we were trying to control our emotions," Jarman said. "But I remember when Keith and I got back after that game against Stanford, one game away from Omaha, we go to our room and we shut the door and we were jumping up and down on the beds like we were on spring break or something."

Western's next hurdle was a second matchup against Florida State, who was playing out of the losers' bracket. With a victory, WCU would be headed to Omaha. Rodney Hennon stepped up with two outs in the bottom of the ninth and hit a shot that looked like a base hit. The tying run was crossing the plate and the winning run was rounding third for the Catamounts, but the Seminole shortstop made a play worthy of a highlight reel and eked out a throw to first base to get Hennon out. FSU won 4–3, and then went on to win the final game 18–3. "We were one win away," said Mike Tidick, who played center field on that team. "If we had just made a couple of plays, we would have gone to Omaha. It's almost like a drug when you get that close."

Roy Hurst, a volatile player who once distinguished himself by breaking the dugout toilet with a bat during a mid-game tantrum, was a freshman on that team and was learning the ropes along with his coach. But he was young and confident, and it never occurred to him that his Catamounts couldn't compete with those big-name teams. "To everyone else it would have been Cinderella, but we didn't pay attention to that," said Hurst, who jokingly ragged LeClair years later about coaching decisions he made during that FSU game. "I wouldn't have been shocked at all."

Through that tumultuous first season, LeClair's players found it easy to forget that their coach was just a few years their senior. Some coaches try to act like their players' peers, White said, but Keith never approached his teams that way. "When you think about it, it was sort of amazing that he could command the respect of those kids when he was twenty-five years old," he said. "He separated himself. He wasn't a buddy-buddy. He kept his distance."

"I never really thought about his age at the time," Tidick said. "He just went out and did his job, kept us believing and kept us working. Keith knew the buttons to push, and he knew the type of player each one of us was. He was just a joy to play for, because you knew he was going to be intense, but if you needed him to put a hand on your shoulder and give you some advice he would do that." Jason Beverlin, who played for LeClair at Western from 1992 to 1994 and later went into college coaching himself, learned as much about leadership from his coach as he did about baseball. "He always had a lot of confidence in me, and that made me so much more confident than I would have been," Beverlin said. "His belief in me made me a lot better than I would have been."

The Catamounts never came quite that close to Omaha again during LeClair's tenure, although they would qualify for NCAA Regionals in 1993 and 1994. During the six seasons Keith served as head coach, they never had a losing season, and they reached the 40-win mark during three of those years. Keith also marked a more significant milestone during that period—he became a father for the first time. Lynn gave birth to their daughter, Audrey, on September 15, 1994.

During their first three years of marriage and even more when they became parents, Lynn was getting a firm grasp on the unique stresses faced by a coach's wife. Keith would often work late nights, and family time on weekends was nonexistent from February through June. She remembers autumn as the best season for quality time with Keith, even if the demands of the job never really ceased for long. But even with countless details before him constantly, Keith was good about leaving the job at the door when he came home. He was an attentive dad, and Lynn has multiple pictures of him asleep on the couch with babies snoozing on his chest.

On the diamond, Keith's teams continued to excel. But he developed a reputation for more than just victories in those days—he became known as the Southern Conference coach most likely to get tossed out of a game. Contrary to his reputation as a quiet, easygoing guy who could get along with anyone from mill worker to college president, LeClair seemed to have trouble locating that diplomacy when he disagreed with an umpire's call. "He had a great temperament with the players. He was a good teacher, a good recruiter," said Fred Cantler, the head trainer at WCU during those years. "But when he started arguing with umpires, he didn't know when to stop. When the umpire would turn and go, Keith would get in front of him. Well, that's when you get tossed."

He started to get ejected from games with such frequency that conference officials had a meeting about it, Cantler said. They wanted to dissuade coaches from such behavior, so they drafted a policy that is still known in the Southern Conference as the "Keith LeClair Rule." The rule dictates that for one ejection, a coach misses one game. If they get ejected twice in a season, they miss four games, and the penalty keeps multiplying.

Matt Stillwell, who played for Keith at WCU from 1994–1998, remembers one game when Keith was thrown out by a certain umpire who repeatedly riled him, and he went out to the equipment shed adjacent to the field and picked up a spike drag, a huge metal tiller-like attachment that they used to drag behind a tractor to clean the field. But that day LeClair addressed his frustration to the equipment, Stillwell said: "He picked up the spike drag over his head, twisted it twice and threw it into a bank. He was so mad."

LeClair's players and friends agree that he mellowed on the diamond as he got older and, particularly, when he became a father. The WCU years were the heyday of his reputation as an argumentative skipper, but he still had flashes of that temper early at East Carolina. And that didn't upset the young men in the dugout. James Molinari, who was on the ECU team in 1999–2000, saw his coach not as a hothead, but as a leader who was not afraid to fight for his players. "That was one of the most endearing qualities he had to us, was that this is the most Christian man who wouldn't hurt a fly, but when one of his players needs to be backed up on a baseball field, he would do anything, he would say anything, he would get in an umpire's face," Molinari said. "So we really respected that about him."

As his reputation for building winning programs spread beyond the Appalachians, LeClair's stock rose as a candidate for coaching vacancies. Randy Mazey was visiting Keith in Cullowhee the day they both learned the East Carolina University job had opened up. Both LeClair and Mazey, an assistant coach at Georgia, decided to apply. East Carolina, located in Greenville in the eastern part of the state, was the third largest college in North Carolina with 17,000 students, and ECU's enrollment was exploding. The school offered a higher salary, a better recruiting budget, and the chance to take lessons learned over a decade in Cullowhee and see how they played with a program that had averaged only twenty-six wins in each of the previous three seasons. Steve White remembers talking over the offer with Keith when East Carolina offered him a contract.

"I remember we went down to Pizza Hut, and he said, 'I want to tell you, they made an offer to me. I don't want to leave,'" White said. "I said, 'Do you feel like you're ready?' And he said, 'I can coach on that level.' He told me what they were offering, and it was good. ECU offered him so much more, program-wise and salary-wise, that we really couldn't do anything."

At home, Lynn was pregnant with their second child, and torn about the idea of leaving the close-knit community that was also just over an hour from her family. The baby was due in August, and ECU officials wanted Keith to start earlier in the summer. He drove back and forth for several weeks so that Lynn could give birth in Cullowhee. One Sunday near her due date, Keith had been there for the weekend and was preparing to drive the six hours back to ECU. Lynn was near tears as she said goodbye, because she felt like she might be starting labor. Keith was already getting consumed by the demands of the new job, and she didn't want to voice her fears, so she watched him back out of the driveway. It turned out their son, J.D., truly was on his way, and Keith got little more that day than a whirlwind tour of North Carolina highways.

"I knew how driven he could be with everything, so I just decided to keep quiet," she said. So he barely got to Greenville before he had to turn around and come back. Jonathan Douglas, called J.D., was born on August 25, 1997. Lynn stayed in Cullowhee long enough to celebrate Audrey's third birthday

Keith relaxes with Audrey and J.D.

in mid-September, then she packed up her young family and undertook the long drive east, anxious about finding her place in the new life Keith had already initiated.

4
Pirate Nation

FROM HIS OFFICE AT EAST CAROLINA, ATHLETIC DIRECTOR
Mike Hamrick was trying to help his newest head coach as-
similate while still deflecting criticism from the Pirate fan
base. During the interview process, Hamrick and his associ-
ates had narrowed the field to five finalists, and one of those
men was Billy Best, a former ECU player and a local favorite.
Another top candidate, Mike Fox, at that time the coach at
North Carolina Wesleyan, went on to become the head coach
at the University of North Carolina, 112 miles to the west.
In that company, LeClair was a relative unknown, and there
was some doubt from the outside about whether he could get
the job done. One anonymous caller even warned Greenville
sportswriter Woody Peele that LeClair was a "hothead who
would embarrass ECU."

"We had some really good quality coaches," Hamrick said
of the finalists. "But in twenty years as a Division I athletic director, and all the opportunities I've had to interview coaches, I've never been more impressed with an individual than I
was with Keith LeClair. I walked out of there saying, 'This is
the guy we're going to hire.'"

LeClair was inheriting a program that typically drew just
fifty fans to its games at Harrington Field. Even though previous coach Gary Overton had led ECU to five NCAA regional
appearances in his thirteen years, the Pirates had finished no
higher than fourth in the conference in his last three seasons.
LeClair's task was to construct a new foundation built on the

work ethic, determination, and fixation on detail that had brought him to this point. The first step he took to that end was the hiring of his assistant coaches.

Randy Mazey, the hunting and fishing buddy who had applied for the ECU post with LeClair, came east as his first assistant, and LeClair took the recommendation of ECU athletic department veterans and brought in former player Tommy Eason as his graduate assistant. His salary budget depleted, Keith liked what Mazey and Eason brought to the table but still felt there was an element missing. He remembered an old timer from nearby Richmond County, a high school coach with forty-two years of experience, who had invited him to speak at his annual baseball clinic a few years earlier. That legendary coach was George Whitfield, and he was now retired and living right there in Greenville.

"I had just gotten over cancer surgery, and the doctor had just cleared me to do more activity," Whitfield said. "Just when I get to feeling better the phone rings, and it's Keith saying, 'I'd like you to come over and help me.' Usually I don't make real quick decisions about things, but for some reason I said, 'Keith, I think I'd really enjoy that.'"

It was one of those quick assessments of character that would pay vast dividends in Keith's life. In a letter he wrote to Whitfield six years later Keith remembered their conversation that day and said, "Never could I have imagined, at that point, the influence you would have on my life. I truly believe God blessed me with your wisdom and presence and because of you I know I am a better man today than I was yesterday." As he prepared for a new challenge after four decades in baseball, Whitfield also learned that he would be volunteering his time, since the NCAA only allowed three salaries for a Division I baseball staff.

Whitfield considers it the best paycheck he never received. "It just goes to show that some of the things in life that mean the most to you have the least price tag put on them," he said.

*July 20, 1997: Keith LeClair is introduced as the eighth
head coach in East Carolina baseball history.*

"If you gave me a million dollars today, I wouldn't trade it for
my experience to know Keith, Lynn, and their families."

From there, the staff turned to the roster they had inher-
ited, players that none of them had recruited but on whom
all were banking to help them make a strong start at ECU.
Cliff Godwin, a native of nearby Snow Hill, North Carolina,
was recruited by Overton and redshirted his first year. He
was anxious for the chance to start his active playing career
when the new coach came to town and took him to lunch.
Godwin was nervous when he sensed LeClair's intensity and
heard his goals for the team. It was a new day for East Carolina baseball, one marked by unlimited potential unlocked
through grueling workouts and complete dedication.

"The expectation level of where the program was going to
go was immediately changed the day he took the job," Godwin said. "We never thought it was possible that East Carolina could go to Omaha and play in the College World Series
until the day he took the job. He made us believe we could
beat anybody on any given day."

If all LeClair had brought to the dugout was a sunny op-
timism and stories about how a mid-major like ECU could
topple the big boys, the following statistic wouldn't be so
dramatic: There were twelve young men, including Godwin,
who began their playing career in purple that fall of 1997.
When LeClair left the program four years later, only Godwin,
Joe Hastings, and Brad Simons remained. The rest had either
left voluntarily, discouraged by the taxing workouts, or had
been cut by the coaches when they seemed unable to help the
Pirates reach their goals.

Lynn LeClair remembers one night in 1998 when her husband was out late. Keith's first team had eked out a 30–29
winning record in the 1998 season, surpassing the .500 milestone only by winning their last six games. She knew her
husband had been frustrated with the Pirates' performance
that winter and spring, and when he came home he told her
that he had been in the office cutting players. When he let a
player go, he always went to great lengths to help him find
another college where he could succeed, and he did whatever
he could to help the young man make that transition, she
said. But to achieve the result he sought, he needed to find
and develop the type of players that could help him get there.
He and Kevin McMullan, who joined his staff in 1999, called
them "grinders."

"They were guys who really appreciated the game and
went about their business in the right way," said McMullan.
"We wanted aggressive offensive players."

"There was a kind of player he looked for, and it was
more your blue-collar type of kid, really tough," Lynn said.
"They're hard-working, and they're not expecting the hand-
outs. They're not soft kids."

Since statistics and raw talent alone were only part of
the picture for Keith, he often took a chance on players
who seemed like unlikely collegiate baseball success stories.
Whitfield remembers the first meeting the new staff ever had

about trimming the roster. The name Bryant Ward came up. Ward, a local boy who had graduated from nearby J.H. Rose High School, later conceded that former Coach Overton had given him a break when he signed him, and that he wasn't recruited by any other schools.

Keith put Ward's name on the table that day in a closed-door session with his coaches. Mazey spoke first and said that Ward should be released. Eason said that he didn't think Ward was ready for Division I baseball, and Whitfield agreed, based on what he had seen from the young man so far. LeClair didn't weigh in about Ward at all, but his name made it to the final roster. And during Ward's sophomore season, he broke into the lineup because of an injury to another player and ended up becoming a key player, even leading the team in batting average and making all-conference his junior year. He went on to become a Division I collegiate assistant coach.

Even with a career that had him just an out away from Omaha on more than one occasion, Keith once said that piecing together a winning record in that 1998 season counted among his greatest coaching accomplishments. "We kind of did that with smoke and mirrors," Mazey said. "Part of what made us competitive is that we had always come from successful winning programs. And a losing season to a coach is kind of the kiss of death."

But with that trying season behind him and a new-look roster stocked with players who bought into the LeClair way, the critics were finally quiet and ownership of ECU baseball seemed to have made a full transfer into Keith's hands. As his second season dawned, Keith got serious about creating a distinct team culture—an environment primed for victory.

In those years, Pirate baseball was characterized first by an absolute focus on making it to Omaha and an attendant emphasis on arduous strength and conditioning. Stories abound from an early morning workout in fall 1999 that featured

Keith waits with Bryant Ward before Ward goes to bat during a Pirate home game at Harrington Field. Ward was the only Pirate who was on the ECU roster from LeClair's first day as coach to his last.

"The Gauntlet"—a military-like obstacle course through the woods that ended with an entire squad of mud-covered athletes. It was the kind of shared experience that reinforced a point LeClair continually drove home to his players—if they can outwork the big schools when the spotlight is off, they can outlast them on the diamond.

"We worked so hard," Godwin said. "We really believed that nobody in the country was outworking us. He demanded a lot, and we really believed that if we worked this hard, we deserved success. Some of the stuff we did in the fall was like Navy Seals stuff."

Ben Sanderson, who started his ECU career in 1999, was struck by his coach's intensity, by the absolute certainty in his voice when he talked about felling the big-name teams and blazing a path to Omaha. And as that culture took hold, those giants started to fall. In 1999, the Pirates compiled a 46–16 record and finished the season ranked in the top twenty-five in three national polls. They earned an invitation to the NCAA Regional in Baton Rouge, where they won their first two games before falling to top-seed and tournament host LSU (it was during that weekend that LeClair first glimpsed a vision of what a top-notch baseball stadium could mean to the ECU program).

The 2000 team defeated North Carolina State, Maryland, and Clemson, and won the Colonial Athletic Association title in its last year as members before heading to Conference USA. Dave Kemble, who became the Pirates' manager in the fall of 1999, had a unique perspective as an observer who was also in the middle of everything the team did. In fact, LeClair told him early on that he wanted him in the huddle for every postgame cheer, when the team would shout "Omaha!"

Kemble could see the players being transformed under the watchful eye of their leader. "If he was a football coach, he would have been like Boise State or Utah: 'We're busting the BCS. We're going to dance with the big boys,'" Kemble said. "And that's what his goal was. We went down to Miami and played them down there, LSU, Clemson. We took them all on. We beat all those teams. They overachieved because they bought into that system."

Much of what made LeClair successful on the baseball diamond would have been as effective in arenas like business or politics. He demanded the same commitment and intensity from each of his players, but he didn't see them all as cogs in the works. Each young man was an individual, and he didn't coach with a "one-size-fits-all" philosophy. Clayton McCullough, a Greenville native who came to ECU in 1999, inspired tough love from Keith. The hometown college hadn't been McCullough's first choice, and when he started out as a walk-on his lack of passion for the program showed, he said.

"He told me that I was the most disappointing player he had ever coached," McCullough said. "At that point, I really wasn't as locked in as I should be. It changed my whole outlook and I knew I needed to grow up some. It was the most important thing I've ever been told."

James Molinari was another young man who had some

growing up to do, and he was an expert at testing the limits of LeClair's patience. Molinari had come to Greenville as a junior transfer from his home state of California, and the East Carolina way of doing things seemed strange to him at first. He showed up at his first practice right on time in a random T-shirt, but all of his teammates had already been there for a half hour, preparing for practice doing a team stretch, dressed in matching assigned practice clothes. The city of Greenville was a culture shock for a West Coast boy, and he resolved to leave ECU after that first season. LeClair could have confronted him harshly, like he did McCullough, but instead LeClair seemed to know that Molinari needed a different approach.

"What I appreciated from him was something that I don't think a lot of coaches would do," Molinari said. "He backed off. I think that he saw that I wasn't happy. I wasn't attending class, and I was violating some rules that, if you violate, you're out of here." LeClair seemed to know that Molinari wasn't really a lazy goof-off; he was dealing with insecurities and struggling to make wise decisions. LeClair kept his distance, careful not to push Molinari away, and the player stayed a Pirate.

Still another distinct brand of psychology was needed for Lee Delfino, a talented Canadian player who was a major recruiting catch but ran afoul of LeClair one day in practice. During a fielding exercise called a square drill, LeClair thought that Delfino was goofing around, and he called him on it. Delfino didn't feel like he deserved correction, he said, so he mouthed off to the coach. The exchange escalated, with LeClair telling Delfino to run and Delfino responding by taking off, skipping the rest of practice.

As Delfino remembers it, he actually skipped the next day of practice too, while he cooled off, but the morning after that missed practice he went to see LeClair and apologized for the incident. He explained that he thought he had been putting forth more effort than Coach recognized during that drill, and LeClair told them that he understood, but that he still couldn't let such a blatant challenge to his authority go without consequences. When Delfino arrived at the field that afternoon for the pregame, he knew that he wouldn't be participating in the typical team warmup. He showed up in turf shoes, headed for the outfield and started running back and forth from one outfield foul pole to the other. More than a decade later, Delfino had no trouble remembering how many times he ran back and forth: eighty-four.

"The lesson was learned," he said. "I actually ran during my batting practice and the opposing team's batting practice. I think it was about two hours." Delfino was too sore to play in the game that day, but coach George Whitfield believes that the ultimate ending to that story came on May 29, 1999, when the Pirates traveled to Louisiana to play in a regional against a legendary Louisiana State University program that had been to the College World Series ten times. The Pirates and the Tigers were tied 10–10 in the bottom of the ninth inning, and Delfino was up. He told his teammates and coaches in the dugout, "I'm going to end this thing," and proceeded to walk out and hit a home run over the fence in front of a packed LSU home stadium. The Pirates eventually lost to LSU in a second meeting and failed to advance in the regional, but Whitfield considers that game "one of the great victories in ECU baseball history."

LeClair was firmly opposed to letting any player—even a recruiting catch like Delfino—become bigger than the program. He emphasized roles to every player, from the superstar starter to the bench warmer—and he made each of them believe that their part could propel the Pirates to a coveted spot in the College World Series. Ben Sanderson was a member of Coach's first recruiting class, and he was redshirted in 1999. In 2000, his first active season, his sole job description was to pinch run for the designated hitter late in the game. "I thought that was the greatest role," Sanderson said. "I would start stretching in the fifth inning, just to get ready to run the bases. He would convince you that your role was the one that was going to get us to the College World Series. And you would believe it."

Coaching alongside Keith, Kevin McMullan felt that Keith's own ascent as a Western Carolina player—from walk-on to all-time hits leader in four years—inspired his boundless hope in players who had done little to earn it except try hard and play tough. He let them know that with unflagging commitment to the team, their chance could come. Joe Hastings, another player from that era who went on to Division I coaching, has often wondered if he would have given himself as many opportunities as Keith afforded him.

LeClair's baseball culture at ECU, steeped in intensity and bent on excellence, produced more than just four consecutive seasons with forty-plus wins. The more enduring result was a group of young men who worked harder than they had ever worked and achieved more than they had ever hoped— together. "I've been in coaching for more than forty-seven years, and never have I ever seen a group of boys as close as during those early years," Whitfield said. "Never."

Molinari still marvels at the improbable friendships that grew out of those years. He was a California boy imbued with a free spirit that ran counter to everything in Keith's diligent New England demeanor, and Molinari collected a whole raft of stories with one central theme: his own rebellious acts, quelled by his coach's common sense and firm hand. There was the time Molinari and teammate Chad Tracy climbed up on the goalposts after the East Carolina football team surprised Miami in a cataclysmic upset in 1999. The two of them were photographed by the Associated Press, and the picture ran all over the country. The photo naturally made its way to the head coach who talked incessantly about the need to represent Pirate baseball with class. At the end of practice one day, Keith held up the newspaper clipping.

"Moli, Chad, what were you thinking?" Keith asked

Molinari recalls: "So we're thinking, 'Oh my God, we're going to have to run. We're going to be running until we throw up.'"

"Did you really think I wouldn't see this?" Keith continued. "Do you really think this is how you're supposed to act as a Division I athlete?"

A self-professed smart aleck, Molinari jumped all the way in with his next comment. "Coach, we saw a bunch of people jumping on the goal post. I was trying to hold it up. I was being a peacemaker." The tension broken, Coach burst out laughing.

"Let's get out of here," he said.

Molinari was also well-known for ordering a beer while in uniform on the way home from a particularly frustrating road trip (LeClair made him send it back), as well as getting into an argument with a wrecker driver who was trying to tow his truck after practice one day (LeClair calmed him down and helped Molinari get his truck back). But it's not stories like those that prompted Molinari to stay in Greenville—the town he originally hated—and become a baseball coach. No fewer than six of his former teammates are coaches, too, and Molinari believes that LeClair cultivated a rare team unity that his Pirate alumni have felt compelled to replicate by leading their own teams.

Of course, Keith was cultivating two families during those years, and the one outside the walls of the baseball stadium made its own sacrifices so that he could pour into the Pirate squad. Lynn was still adjusting to the realities of life as a coach's wife, and she had never worn the "baseball wife" persona comfortably. She brought the kids to the field often to see their daddy—one of them would often ride around the bases on his shoulders after a game—but she wasn't into the intricacies of the sport itself, and she was happy when he kept

his coaching life separate. She devoted her energy to helping the kids find their place and making connections with
people outside of the baseball stadium, and she modeled that
balance for Keith when the intricacies of the dugout and the
diamond threatened to engulf him.

"Weekends, that was the killer, because baseball really
consumes the weekend," she said. "When you look out and
everybody else has family time, and you don't, that was really
hard." But Keith was an attentive dad when he was home,
worried about the kids' safety and conscientious about their
needs. As newlyweds, the LeClairs had become regulars at a
church in Cullowhee, and in Greenville they made church
selection a priority. They started attending Oakmont Baptist
Church and joined a Sunday school class there, leading to
enduring friendships with families in the congregation who
had young kids the same ages as Audrey and J.D.

Mary Ann Cooper and Lynn had an instant bond because
their kids were the same ages at the same preschool, and
they were lifelines to one another. They spent time together
nearly every day. Mary Ann's husband, Nelson, and Keith
would become close friends too, but Nelson remembers a
puzzling first impression. The Coopers were invited to the
LeClairs' for dinner, but Keith got home from work late, after
the guests were already there. The wives and children were
in other parts of the house, and Nelson introduced himself,
hoping to get to know Keith a little bit.

"He sat down, and he didn't say much at all," Nelson
Cooper said. "He immediately cut on *Sports Center*, and he
looked at me and said, 'You don't mind if I watch this, do
you?' It was the most fascinating meeting."

Not too long after that, Keith invited Nelson to ride with
him to Raleigh on a recruiting trip, and the two got to talk
about deeper things. In September 1999, when the massive
Hurricane Floyd came through Greenville, the two families
bunkered together at the ECU baseball field house, convinced

that it was a safer structure than either of their homes.

The storm, which came right on the heels of the smaller Hurricane Dennis, led to the most devastating flood in the history of Eastern North Carolina. The flood did $1.6 billion of damage in Pitt County, where ECU was located, and thousands of people were left homeless by the rising waters. One of those was Jerry Greene, East Carolina baseball's resident superfan and a close friend of Keith's. The two got to know each other in Keith's early days as head coach when Jerry stopped by and told him that he hadn't missed a Pirate game in four years and he hoped to continue that streak. "I used to joke with Keith: "What are you going to do when I miss a game?" Greene said. "He would say, 'I'm going to call you a fair-weather fan.' And I would say, 'You can't take another job until I miss a game.'"

When Jerry and his wife Melanie were forced to vacate their house because the flood had deposited ten feet of water there, discussions between Jerry and Keith turned from baseball to more practical subjects. Keith would call often to check on the Greenes, who were forced to live in a tiny camper for six months after Floyd. One time about two weeks before Christmas, Keith called Jerry and asked him if they would like to stay at the LeClairs' house in Greenville while the LeClairs spent the holidays with Lynn's family in South Carolina.

Much was in place for Keith and his family leading up to that 2001 Super Regional against Tennessee. The LeClairs were happy with their church and friends and their kids were settling into school and activities. Keith had been impaired by severe back pain that led to surgery on a ruptured disk during the 2000 season, but a year later he was dieting and exercising more than he had in years.

Professionally, the East Carolina team had gone 47–13 that season for Keith's best record as a Pirate, won the CAA title, and been ranked eleventh in the national postseason polls.

And all of those wins weren't going unnoticed in the larger Division I programs. A couple of high-profile schools were already penciling Keith LeClair's name in on their short list of head coaching candidates. By any gauge of coaching success, he was at the top of his game.

The 2001 Pirates, the last team LeClair was able to coach all the way through the season. LeClair, who would be diagnosed with ALS less than a month after this photo was taken, is second from left in the front row.

5
Diagnosis

BETWEEN MONTHS OF BACK PAIN AND SURGERY AND THE mounting demands of coaching and family, Keith had let himself get out of shape, he told Lynn and his friends. In the fall of 2000 and early in the '01 season, he set a goal—to get back to his college playing weight. Once resolved, he applied his usual drive to his personal regimen—eating only healthy food and spending any spare moments in the weight room and on the treadmill. After a few months of this, everyone around him started to see dramatic results.

"He just kept losing and losing and losing," Lynn said. "I was thinking, 'Is he anorexic? What is going on with him?' I had never seen him that way. The weight was just really coming off."

Everyone knew that Keith had been working to slim down, but as the season went on some friends shared Lynn's concern that he was taking it too far. In retrospect, the weight loss was a grim harbinger that had nothing to do with fitness or diet.

Just about every spring Keith touched base with his old high school coach Hank Beecher, to check in and to inquire whether Beecher had any outstanding players that Keith might consider for East Carolina. Hank remembers part of their 2001 conversation quite vividly, after he asked his former player if he was still lifting weights. "Yeah," LeClair replied, "But my workouts haven't been good. Maybe because I'm tired or something."

Nelson Cooper and his wife Mary Ann, some of the Le-Clairs' first friends in Greenville, had moved to Clemson in 2000, and in April of 2001 they returned to Greenville to visit, staying with the LeClairs. It was a busy weekend, full of baseball games and spring football events, and Keith seemed preoccupied. Even so, in past years the two couples would have stayed up after putting the kids to bed to catch up. But that weekend, even though Keith wanted that quality time, the thirty-five-year-old seemed depleted of energy. "Both those nights, I remember it clear as day, he would sit down for just a minute, and then he would say, 'I'm really tired,'" Nelson Cooper recalled. "Here's a guy that looked like he was in the best shape of his life, and he couldn't stay up to talk."

As the 2001 regular season closed and the postseason heated up, signs that something was amiss with Coach's health seemed to multiply. Team manager Dave Kemble recalls sitting across from Keith in the locker room, after the coach had been throwing batting practice, and noticing spasms in his shoulder or his arm. It had to be the heat, Kemble thought, or the intensity of throwing batting practice. Former Pirate Cliff Godwin, on a break from playing pro ball in St. Louis, went to visit Keith in his office and recalls that LeClair mentioned a doctor's appointment he had made, to ask about muscle spasms in his left shoulder.

And immediately after that heartbreaking Super Regional against Tennessee, LeClair went to the place where he could always unwind the best—his in-laws' home in the hill country of South Carolina. Bill Carson, the East Carolina track and field coach and a good friend of LeClair's, was at his own mountain place and met Keith for a fishing outing. Keith would cast, then rub his left arm, cast, then rub his arm again. "What's wrong?" Carson asked. "My arm's been bothering me bad since I threw BP before the last game at Tennessee."

The closest eyewitness to each of these worrisome

*Coaches George Whitfield, Keith LeClair, and Kevin
McMullan stand for pregame ceremonies before a
February home matchup against New York Tech. Before
long, Keith watched many games from a van outside
the first base line fence, and in mid-April he sat in the
dugout for one last time at UNC-Charlotte.*

developments was, of course, Lynn, and she clung to the idea
that it was just stress. Even her father Doug, who knew Keith
better than just about anyone, attributed his symptoms to the
emotional rigors of his coaching responsibilities. But Keith
himself seemed to know that something more serious was
going on, and when he told his wife that he was concerned,
Lynn surrendered to worry for the first time.

ECU head athletic trainer Mike Hanley had recommended that the LeClairs visit a local doctor, and that June they
left the kids with a babysitter and went to what would be the
first of many appointments. The doctor ran Keith through
a battery of tests and asked him a lot of questions about his
symptoms. Of special concern to the doctor were Keith's left

arm and his tongue, which was losing its muscular function. It all seemed like much ado about nothing to Lynn, who had barely noticed the gradual changes because she saw Keith every day. Even when the doctor said she suspected it could be a disease known as ALS, it seemed like a surreal possibility.

But then the doctor dropped the bombshell. Lynn recalled, "When we left there, she basically told us that if we didn't have a good life insurance policy that we might want to check into it. And by this time, I'm sort of coming unglued. We both left in tears. It was like somebody had died already."

The preliminary diagnosis was amyotrophic lateral sclerosis, also known as ALS or Lou Gehrig's disease for the famous major league baseball player who died of the illness in 1941. ALS causes the progressive degeneration of the nerve cells that affect the brain and spinal cord. The damage to those nerve cells robs the body's muscles of needed stimulation, causing them to atrophy and often leading to gradual paralysis. According to the ALS Association, half of all people diagnosed with the disease die within three years of diagnosis and 80 percent within five years. Although a small percentage of cases are linked to a genetic predisposition, most ALS patients never know what causes the disease to strike. It has no known cure, and no effective treatment has been discovered.

Keith and Lynn knew almost none of those facts yet, and they were a couple united in their dislike and detachment from anything medical. Shell-shocked, they went home and tried to speak normally to the kids and the babysitter. Suddenly, Lynn, who hardly knew how to turn the family's computer on, was starved for information about this intruder, and Mary Ann Cooper started spending hours on the phone with her while Mary Ann looked up facts on the internet.

Meanwhile, as the LeClairs' personal life was being ravaged by the prospect of ALS, Keith's career star had never shined brighter. Just before that doctor's visit, he got a call from the athletic director at the University of Florida, asking him to come to Tallahassee and interview for their head coaching vacancy. Even though Florida was a much bigger program, Keith felt loyal to East Carolina and dedicated to following through on his plan for a new Pirate baseball stadium, so he said no to the Gators. ECU offered him a five-year contract extension, and he signed it.

Then the University of Georgia called, and that prospect was much more attractive than Florida because of its proximity to Lynn's family in South Carolina. Lynn wanted him to pursue the Georgia job, but right at that time they also got his diagnosis, and then the Georgia officials called to say that they were planning to offer the job to another candidate. But that wasn't the end of it, because Georgia called back to say that their number one pick had turned them down and Keith was again their top prospect. Through all of those conversations, though, health concerns had taken a front seat, and Keith knew that he couldn't make a move. "There was just too much going on," Lynn said. "He ended up saying, 'I'm sorry. I can't pursue this right now.'"

As reluctant as the LeClairs were to give voice to this shattering label that had been put on Keith, they knew they had to tell their loved ones something. A series of difficult phone calls to friends and family followed. Lynn and Keith balanced the news of the doctor's opinion with their own fervent hopes that he was actually sick with something far less serious. To many loved ones, that phone call or conversation was a cataclysmic life event that stood out in their memories for years.

Jack Leggett was on the field at Clemson, overseeing a summer baseball camp, when his cell phone rang. It was Lynn, bearing the report of Keith's diagnosis and, for Jack, a burden of sadness that would become a permanent part of him. He tried to get his mind around this news about the young coach who was so much like a son to him. And he wished, at that moment, that he had not learned so much about ALS during his years at WCU. "I had some experience with it with Bob Waters having it at Western Carolina," Leggett said. "I had seen it, I had felt it, I had watched it. So when she told me that, it crushed me.

"And I remember just going 'No, no, no, no.' It was a hot day, and I was underneath these trees, there were kids at the camp all over the place, and I remember, underneath one of those big oak trees just crying, just crying as hard as I could cry, just going, 'No, this can't be right.'"

Todd Raleigh, Keith's former teammate at Western Carolina who was hired to succeed his friend as the Catamounts' head coach, talked to Keith three times a week about coaching, recruiting, and their families. They saw each other in Durham just after the 2001 season, and he remembers telling LeClair, "You look like hell." Just weeks later, the man who had inspired Raleigh to become a coach was calling with news of a devastating illness. "I never saw that coming in a million years," Raleigh said.

The Pirate baseball players were scattered all over the country, many playing ball in summer leagues in Cape Cod or the Great Lakes area. Word started to trickle out that Coach was sick with ALS, a prospect that seemed impossible for their strong, strapping leader. "We had a joke that he was pound for pound the strongest coach out there, because he would lift with us in the weight room, and he would put us all to shame," said James Molinari, who had graduated from ECU but was still living in Greenville. "If he could suit up and put on a uniform, he would have been the best player on the team right then and there. So it put a perspective on everyone's mortality."

Bryant Ward, the only ECU player who was with LeClair from his first day as coach to his last, was playing summer ball when he got a phone call from his mother with the news. When he returned to campus, he was stunned by the physical changes and the deterioration of speech that were already affecting LeClair. "He's in the prime of his career, and we're a bunch of college kids who go play summer ball for two months. We come back and all of a sudden he's having trouble making out a word," Ward said. "In college you don't really think about any of that stuff. And the people who are a little older and a little smarter, they try to warn you, but it just kind of smacks you in the face."

That summer commenced a roller coaster ride for the LeClairs that jerked them in and out of conflicting diagnoses and visits to specialists in three different states. An avid hunter, Keith knew that he could have been bitten by a tick, and their research indicated that Lyme's disease can often exhibit ALS-like symptoms. That prospect fanned hope for them, and they saw a doctor at Baptist Hospital in Winston-Salem who was unable to rule out either disease. They also traveled to Johns Hopkins Medical Center in Baltimore and to a Lyme's disease specialist in Missouri, but none of them yielded much new information, and all fueled LeClair's "mediphobia"—doctors with lukewarm bedside manner, confusing and impersonal hospitals.

"We were just kind of trying anything," Lynn reflected. "But at some point Keith was like, 'OK, I'm done with this. We'll just go back home.'"

Most people with ALS find a physician who specializes in treatment of the illness, but the LeClairs were weary of strange doctors, and back in Greenville they asked Dr. Rick Figler to oversee Keith's care. Figler was a family physician with a sports medicine background, but his greatest qualification was that the LeClairs trusted him. Figler resolved to learn all he could about ALS to steer his patient through the uncertainty ahead. House calls to the LeClair home became part of his routine, and when he couldn't visit he was checking in with Keith by phone.

In New Hampshire, Kevin LeClair and his sisters felt disbelief that the one who was stricken was their younger brother, the athlete who had made all Walpole proud with his strength and determination. Former teammates, friends, and coaches from New Hampshire and Western started calling each other, trying to glean information, and for Beecher it was a bombshell that seemed impossible. One thing stands out to him about the conversations he had with his former player after the diagnosis, though—Beecher saw in Keith a steadfast Christian faith that seemed to have deepened since his teenage years.

"He mentioned many times his faith in God, and that no matter what happens He would see him through," Beecher said. "And that's the biggest thing I remember from the post-diagnosis conversations. I had known that he was into the church, but I didn't know that it was that big of a part of his life."

Keith's family did not attend church regularly when he was growing up, but he was exposed to Christianity at the Denny Doyle Baseball Camp in high school and later when he moved to the Bible Belt to attend college at Western. Catamount teammate Keith Shumate recalls Keith LeClair asking him what he believed about Jesus one day as they walked down the hill from the cafeteria. "He asked me what I believed, and I said that I believed that Jesus had died on the cross for us, and that I had accepted him as my personal Savior. He told me that day, 'I believe the exact same thing.'" Around that time, LeClair's friend Todd Cottrell—the Western Carolina quarterback—spoke with Keith often about the hope he had found in Christianity, and later LeClair credited Cottrell with helping him see the need to put Christ first in his life.

Back in Cullowhee after his foray into the minor leagues, Keith started attending Cullowhee Baptist Church, and he entered comfortably into the life of the congregation. He had a deep respect for the church's pastor, Joe Yelton, who baptized him during a service in 1991. Yelton also conducted Keith and Lynn's wedding ceremony the following year. The LeClair family stayed active in Cullowhee Baptist until they moved to Greenville, where they quickly discovered

Oakmont Baptist and found it one of the anchors of their life in a new city.

Sherry Odom was teaching adult Sunday School at Oakmont during those years, and as part of her ministry she would visit newcomers and invite them to Sunday School. As she got to know the LeClairs inside their home and they agreed to join her class, a friendship blossomed that would become one of the most important either family had ever had. And the irony of their connection, Sherry Odom said, was the fact that neither she nor her husband Mike knew much of anything about East Carolina baseball.

"We were not the typical Greenville baseball family," she said. "That was what was so odd about our relationship, was that we were so completely different. They were all about baseball, and we were not about baseball, and honestly the only common ground we had was the Lord."

The Coopers, who were also Oakmont Baptist friends, had certain expectations about coaches and their limitations on being involved at church. Steve Logan, then the head football coach at East Carolina, was also a member of the congregation, and everyone there knew of the stringent demands on coaches' time, especially on weekends. That's why Nelson Cooper was so surprised to see Keith attend the early service by himself on a spring weekend when Lynn and the kids were on a trip to South Carolina.

"We were all pretty accustomed that during the season, you just didn't see coaches at church," he said. "I was ushering that morning, and in comes Keith, walking by himself. And I thought, 'You've got a hundred reasons no one expects you to be here this morning. You had a game last night—it went extra innings. You've got a game this afternoon. And you're coming to church.'" Years later, when the gravity of Keith's illness became apparent, Nelson thought back to that morning and his friend's growing faith and felt sure that the Lord was preparing Keith for the trials ahead. LeClair was seeking spiritual nourishment back then, he said, with no knowledge of how much he would soon need that sustenance.

Chuck Young and his family came to Greenville in 1998 with the vision of starting a ministry called Sportworks that would minister to East Carolina athletes. One of the first coaches he visited was Keith. Logan had already given Chuck carte blanche to work with the football players, and he received similar encouragement from LeClair about ministering to the baseball team. When Young stopped by his office, he noticed a Christian magazine on the table, and LeClair welcomed him warmly. "He embraced it very much from the beginning," Young said.

Clearly, all of those milestones on Keith's faith journey loomed large in the summer of 2001, when his mortality dramatically took center stage in his life. Through most of their marriage, Lynn had been encouraged by his interest in Christianity, but she always felt like the one who knew more about the Bible, the one teaching the children about God. Baseball was just too consuming, she felt, for Keith to give much time to spiritual pursuits. Then he was diagnosed, and she watched a different side of him emerge.

"During that time, he was just in the Bible all the time," she said of that summer and fall. "He was really taking it in. And people were asking him to speak at different places, too. He was just taking in the Bible in leaps and bounds. And at the same time, it's like our lives are falling apart. We were knowing that what we're looking at was impossible, but at the same time we were holding onto the fact that maybe it could be something else, or maybe it could be healed. We were holding on to all of these things: faith growing, faith fragile."

"I think he was trying to find some understanding of it," Dave Kemble said. "Not, 'Why me?' but it was, 'OK, you've given me this, now what do I do with it?'"

As their faith was forged in the flames of ALS, the LeClairs held fast to the hope that Keith would be healed of the disease. Even though conventional wisdom says that a cure for ALS doesn't exist, they wanted to carry a different message: That their God is bigger than any medical prognosis or deadline. "It was tough for me, because in reality there were two camps on this thing," said Nelson Cooper, who heard the faith-based healing beliefs alongside the medical realities that defined ALS. "They were our close friends, and we shared a sense of faith with them. We wanted to stand as friends with them and say we're going to fight it. But ALS is about like pancreatic cancer. When you hear those words, I don't know anybody who had made it."

Whether or not healing came, Keith resolved to trust God on this new and terrifying journey, and he jumped at an opportunity to tell his church family of that conviction on August 19, 2001. Before that fateful first doctor's visit, Lynn could hardly have imagined her husband speaking openly about his faith in front of hundreds of people, but that day he seemed born to bear witness to God's work in his life. He told the congregation that in the twelve years since he had become a Christian, he had believed in God but had not put his faith first. When he was diagnosed, he said, he dove into prayer and Scripture but felt overcome by guilt for all of the time he had relegated Christ to a back seat.

"I asked Him to forgive me for being self-centered and not putting Him number one in my life," he said. "And He spoke to me, and He gave me a sense of peace. He answered a lot of those prayers, He spiritually healed me. I really believed that. I just feel that, through these trials that I have, He wants me to glorify Him. He wants me to lift Him up."

Unfortunately, even though he would give a handful of other speeches that fall, from Raleigh to South Carolina, Keith's public speaking days were coming to an end almost before they started. ALS can either originate in the lower body or the upper body, and in the latter situation—which was Keith's—deterioration of speech and respiratory function is quite rapid. ECU players who had left Greenville for the summer were shocked when they returned and heard Coach—who had last been encouraging them with an eloquent post-game speech—struggling to form his words. By fall, Lynn said, Keith would not attempt to eat in public for fear that he would choke, and his arm strength was already faltering so much that Lynn had to carry all of the luggage on a fall trip to see a specialist in Missouri.

"It was surreal in the sense that you would almost think, 'OK, it's going to stop here. It's not going to keep getting worse,'" Molinari said. "The first thing was his speech, but also he would hit fungoes and you could see that he was struggling to swing the fungo bat. He would throw BP, and normally he's so effortless in throwing, and it looked like the ball was a shot put in his hand. Those things were just very tough to see."

For Kemble, the team manager who had made a habit out of stopping by Coach's office to shoot the breeze, the changes were so dramatic that he found himself rushing past Keith's office, or just poking his head in and saying, "Hey, Coach," as if on his way somewhere else. It was awkward for Kemble when he didn't understand what Coach was saying, and his defense mechanism was to avoid him. But Keith's emotional insights were razor-sharp, even if his articulation wasn't, and he caught on to Kemble's evasiveness fast.

"I remember later in the fall, I tried to do that again, and he called me into his office," Kemble said. "He said he understood where I was coming from, and he said, 'Don't avoid me.' He said he had seen that from a lot of different people. From that point on, I felt more comfortable with him."

After a whirlwind summer packed with medical questions and unsettling doctor's visits, a semblance of routine returned when the players reported back for fall drills. As the young men tried to absorb the physical changes in their coach, Keith and his assistants did whatever they could to get down to business. "He told us, 'I don't want pity. I don't want you guys to ask me about this every day. I'm going to continue to expect a lot from you, and don't expect any less from me,'" Ben Sanderson recalled.

The other three members of Keith's staff—Tommy Eason, Kevin McMullan, and George Whitfield—sought to strike the balance between helping Keith in areas that might present a struggle for him and stepping back enough to maintain his leadership of the team. "We said, 'Nothing's going to change. We're just going to do our job, and he's going to get to the bottom of it,'" McMullan remembered. Keith was comprehensible and mobile enough that fall to fulfill most of his duties—he was still driving to work every day—although he and Lynn decided he should stop driving when the kids were in the car.

But from his office at the East Carolina field house, Keith was pouring his energy into more than just offseason conditioning and player evaluations. The spiritual awakening that had accompanied his diagnosis was influencing every aspect of his life, and colleagues like Devin O'Neill, then the ECU men's soccer coach, were transformed by watching him put one foot in front of the other despite such a devastating prognosis.

"When Keith got sick, and how he handled everything, just the depth of his faith, the courage, and just the calm, it was just incredibly powerful," O'Neill said. "It was just something to watch that you said, 'That's for real. And that's what I want.' Keith was just so strong, and at every opportunity he would talk about his faith and what it meant to him." O'Neill began to ask LeClair questions about his faith and how it changed his perspective, and that fall, through Keith's influence and his own wife's growing faith, he made a commitment to follow Jesus.

Over Thanksgiving break that year, Keith spoke at another

church—Nelson and Mary Ann Coopers' congregation in Pendleton, South Carolina. In his talk to First Baptist Church, he again told his story and encouraged his listeners to put their faith first. But public speaking was getting much more taxing, and baseball season was still ahead. The old year had already brought the LeClairs so far from normal that they could barely recognize their old life. But Keith and his loved ones couldn't even conceive of the tests 2002 would bring.

6

Final Season

BASEBALL PEOPLE FIND COMFORT IN THE MINUTIAE OF THE game, and early in 2002 Keith, his staff, and his players took refuge in pitch counts, batting averages, and on-base percentages. The schedule, set long before the detonation in their lives, started with a home sweep of Delaware and featured early road trips to Cincinnati and Alabama-Birmingham. The roster included the blue-collar talent typical of LeClair's squads but lacked some of the power of the previous team that had come so close to Omaha. As much as they possibly could, Eason and McMullan tried to defer to LeClair's leadership about daily coaching decisions that winter, but collaboration became more difficult as his speech and mobility lessened.

Game-time coaching decisions often have to be made quickly, former ECU assistant Tommy Eason said, so the staff came up with ways to include Keith's input even when he couldn't chime in right away. The assistants would choose two pitchers to send to the bullpen, instead of only one, and then ask Keith which pitcher should enter the game in relief.

Keith was still trying to speak, but he also carried a small computer into the dugout, a device that allowed him to type out messages to the people around him. He also started writing encouraging notes to the players in lieu of conversations. As the season wore on, though, he started having to miss practice more, and he wasn't there to take a player's day-to-day pulse—to assess his confidence at the plate, for instance.

Keith had always looked for players who had an edge on a certain day, an edge that might not even be perceptible to most observers. It became harder and harder for him to make those distinctions for himself.

"That was the sad part, was when Kevin [McMullan] and I had to start making some decisions even when he was sitting there," Eason said. "And I think Keith understood it, more so than anybody. Whether you think it or not, he was still coaching. There was no doubt about it. But there were times, when it got toward the end of his coaching career, and we had to make decisions on who's going to start the game."

Once that year, about a dozen games into the season, Le-Clair asked McMullan to make a lineup change. The adjustment didn't work out well, and it was a major factor in the Pirates' loss that day. After the game, McMullan stood up and apologized to the players for making the decision that Keith, had in fact, made. But Keith refused to let his assistant coach take the fall, and he owned up to the mistake. Later, he made it clear to McMullan that his illness didn't absolve him of any responsibility, and he wasn't interested in making any excuses. Coach Mac, as he was known on the team, took that cue and never again used Keith's ALS as a crutch or even as a motivational tool. "Some people might have used it as motivation, but we never did," McMullan said. "He wouldn't want it that way, and it's not honest with the kids."

When they did talk to the players about Keith's ALS, they framed it not as game-day inspiration but as an opportunity to learn how to live. There were times of sadness and times when none of them wanted to face Coach as his health deteriorated, but they were the privileged few who got to have inside access to his courage and perseverance as he faced the unknown. "We tried to sell it to them every day that you're going through something that you'll be able to share with people every day," McMullan said. "We'd say, 'This is going to change you guys. This is a wonderful opportunity.'"

While the Pirate baseball family was witnessing Keith's decline every day, his New Hampshire family had trouble grasping what was happening to him. His brother Kevin and his sister Sharlene were concerned and in mid-March they decided to drive from New Hampshire to Norfolk, Virginia, to watch East Carolina play against Old Dominion University. For years they had watched their brother coach but focused on the players and the outcome. That night they could only watch the coach. Kevin had gone to North Carolina to see Keith twice after his diagnosis, but the last time had been five months earlier, and he was stunned by the change. Keith's neck muscles were too weak to support his head well, he was way too thin, and he was using a portable suction machine to clean out the saliva that collected because he couldn't swallow effectively.

"It was absolutely shocking to me," Kevin said. "He just looked like this weathered old man who couldn't hold his head up. He looked like he had aged thirty years."

Along with loss of speech and arm strength, Keith's swallowing function was so impaired that eating solid food became both difficult and hazardous for him. Lynn was always nearby, and she performed the Heimlich maneuver on her husband so many times that it became almost routine. That February the LeClairs reluctantly went to Pitt County Memorial Hospital in Greenville so that Keith could have a feeding tube placed surgically into his stomach through his abdominal wall. It was one of the first major concessions to the ALS that Keith and Lynn had to make, and Sherry Odom watched their stubbornness with a bit of foreshadowing because, as a physical therapist, she knew some of the hurdles that were ahead. But as anyone close to the LeClairs knew, they were not going to be coerced into giving up any of Keith's freedoms until they were ready.

"It was exhausting, because I could see in my mind's eye what was coming, like the lift and the wheelchair and all of those things, and of course they would not accept them until the time came," Odom said. "Which to me, as a therapist, was frustrating, because I wanted it to be easier for them, but there was no easy route. It really helped me to see how all of this has to unfold in each person's own time."

Sherry was one of the few medical professionals whom the LeClairs trusted implicitly, and because they wanted her to help with so many aspects of Keith's care she educated herself on procedures far outside the realm of her expertise. When Keith wasn't comfortable with the person working on him, he had his ways of making that clear and claiming his rights as a patient, she remembered.

One respiratory therapist learned that the hard way in the winter of 2002, when he was trying to suction Keith's lungs shortly after he got the feeding tube. The therapist decided to suction Keith through the nose, but Keith didn't approve of that decision. "He starts to put that tube in Keith's nose, and Keith couldn't use his arms, but he had legs," she said. "He put his foot up on the guy's chest and pushed him across the room."

By April 10, the Pirates were 24–1–8 and gearing up for a road trip to conference rival UNC-Charlotte, a team that featured future major-league pitcher John Main. Dave Kemble, the Pirates' manager, vividly recalls the third game of that series, on a scorching-hot afternoon in a stadium called Knight's Castle. Up to that point, Keith had been watching the action from a van situated just outside the fence parallel to the right-field line, because the hard bench and the heat in the dugout had become too uncomfortable for him.

But that day Lynn approached Kemble before the game and said that Keith really wanted to watch from the dugout. "So she drove him around, and she wanted me to come down and walk with him," Kemble said. "At this point he could still walk—he had really good use of his legs—but his upper body was going. And it was as hot a day in April as you'll ever see around here. And he wanted to be in that dugout so badly."

Kemble helped Keith get settled on the bench, and the first ECU batter, Jamie Paige, took his stance, facing Main and his explosive fast ball. Paige fouled a ball off straight behind him, right over the Pirate dugout. Everyone inside, sure it was coming their way, ducked or dodged; everyone, that is, except Keith, who could no longer move that fast. McMullan, always quick to joke around with Keith, grinned at him and declared, "Every man for himself!" Keith and everyone nearby broke out laughing, but soon after that foul Eason handed Kemble a glove and gave him one responsibility: Stay near Keith for the whole game and catch any ball that comes near him. It would be the last dugout view LeClair would ever have, and later, friends would wonder if Keith knew what was coming when he insisted on moving from the air conditioning into the sweltering heat.

The LeClairs loaded into their van that Sunday afternoon for the four-hour drive back to Greenville, and from the first miles Keith seemed weak and disoriented. Lynn stopped to give him some fluids through the feeding tube and then focused on the long trip ahead. Audrey had school the next day, so Lynn didn't want to get home too late. When they pulled into the garage after dark, she realized that Keith was in worse shape than she had ever seen him. He walked to the downstairs bathroom, and she sent Audrey upstairs to start her bath.

As Lynn was unloading the car, Keith had an accident in the bathroom, and she realized that he had no control over his bowels. She told him to go upstairs to shower and he walked toward the front door instead. "And he's just looking at me," she said. "Then he starts upstairs, and I remembered, 'He can't get his shirt off. So I go running back up the stairs, and as I started to help him with his shirt, he just kind of fell over on me. I somehow got him into the rocking chair, and his head fell back. His face looked gray to me, and at that point I picked up the phone and called 9-1-1. I don't have a clue what I said."

Keith was literally dying from lack of oxygen, the ALS having so damaged his respiratory system that he could no longer breathe effectively. When the ambulance arrived, the paramedics hooked him up to oxygen and took him to Pitt County Memorial Hospital. Lynn followed in the van after she got Audrey settled at the neighbors' house (J.D. had gone to South Carolina with his grandparents after the game.) When she arrived, the nurses told her that Keith had initially resisted the IV they tried to start, but they had eventually hooked it up and started him on fluids. At that point Lynn was convinced that Keith was only severely dehydrated.

The truth dawned on her the next day, when the doctors came into his room and began talking to the LeClairs about putting him on a ventilator, a portable machine that would deliver oxygen directly to his lungs. Medical terms were flying around, and Lynn was trying to grasp the gravity of the situation—that Keith would die without the vent. She could see on the monitor that Keith's oxygen levels were dropping lower and lower. In the middle of this, Mike Odom came by with the LeClairs' tax forms to get Lynn's signature and left to go mail the forms. Next was Joyce Stroud, the ECU football secretary, who had a salad for Lynn's lunch. Lynn's parents had started the six-hour drive back to Greenville to be with her, but they were still en route.

Because the LeClairs weren't ready to make a quick decision about surgically implanting the ventilator, the doctor intubated Keith through the mouth as a temporary measure. But the medical professionals knew that he had reached a point where he would no longer be able to breathe on his own. Lynn and Keith both felt resistant to the idea of the vent, both because things seemed to be happening too fast and because Keith had never thought that he would want to be kept alive by artificial means. Conversations ensued about bringing the kids up to see him if the LeClairs refused the vent, so that they could say goodbye. Audrey and J.D. actually came up in the elevator, and then were sent down again when the decision was made to go ahead with surgery that would implant the endotracheal tube into Keith's throat. The tube was attached to the ventilator that would become Keith's constant companion.

"We were completely unprepared for all of it," Lynn said. "We didn't even know what the next step was. I remember being out in the hallway with Rick [Figler, Keith's regular doctor], and saying, 'If it were just the two of us, maybe, I could see it, but with the kids I feel like we need to do whatever we can do.'"

Chuck Young, who had become a spiritual mentor of sorts to Keith, was in the hospital room that day as the LeClairs grappled with an unbelievable decision. He felt at the time that Keith didn't want to go on the vent, but that Lynn wasn't ready to let go. Amid tubes, beeping machines, rushing nurses, medical jargon, and income tax forms, the LeClair family was being asked to disentangle God's sovereignty from their own desires and the possibilities offered by advanced medical science. In the end, Keith was convinced that God still had things for him to do.

Some who knew Keith well couldn't help but question that decision initially. One of the things that drew ECU groundskeeper Joey Perry to LeClair when they became friends in 2000 was the coach's uncommon inner strength and independence. He was reluctant even to hire a professional groundskeeper back then, because he preferred to do all of the mowing and field work himself. Later, when Keith got sick, he used to tell Perry that he wouldn't want to be kept alive by a machine. So, like many others, Perry went to the hospital that day to say goodbye. Jack Leggett and Todd Raleigh drove through the night from upstate South Carolina for the same reason. "I honestly thought that was it," Raleigh said. "When we left, we thought it was the last time we would ever see him."

"He had told me that he wasn't going to do that [go on a vent], and when it happened I was questioning it, because I didn't know if I would have done that," Perry said. "But I think it turned out to be a blessing for everybody. You don't ever know, when you're faced with that situation, what you're going to do."

After the vent was put in, the LeClairs had to stay in the hospital for three weeks while they learned how to care for the machine. Lynn was subject to detailed instructions about suctioning and cleaning and caring for the vent. "You think bringing home a baby was somewhat traumatic the first time. This was way beyond," Chuck Young remembered. It marked a major loss of independence for Keith and the end of his ability to communicate verbally. As the speech therapy supervisor for the hospital, Stuart Robertson volunteered to work with the LeClairs. When she walked into their room for the first time, she knew nothing about East Carolina baseball or Coach LeClair. But their bond was immediate, and Robertson became such a trusted helper that Keith introduced her to others as his guardian angel.

Robertson told the LeClairs about a one-way valve that could keep Keith on the ventilator but still allow him to speak for short periods of time. She set him up so that he could speak again, but his speech was so impaired from the ALS that he only asked her to do that two more times after that day in the hospital room. "He could talk, but it didn't sound like his voice, and he didn't like the sound of it," Robertson said. "But Lynn wanted to hear his voice, and the kids wanted to hear him say, 'I love you.'"

When the LeClairs were discharged, they left with a communication board that Robertson had made for Keith. His hands were strong enough that he could point to the letters, and he spelled so fast it was hard to keep up with him, she said. It wouldn't be long after he got home when he lost so much function in his hands that he had to use his feet for a modified letter-board that sat on the floor. He was still walking when he left the hospital, and he wouldn't even consider Robertson's suggestion that he ride out to the van in a wheelchair. The wheelchair served a different function. "The ventilator rode in the wheelchair and he walked out," she explained.

Through all this, Keith was still the East Carolina baseball coach, and university athletic officials set aside funds to help with the expenses of his treatment. During their long hospital stay, ECU had arranged for a first-floor expansion of the LeClairs' house so that Keith could have his own wheelchair-accessible room. Lynn set out to learn her new daily tasks, from keeping Keith's new artificial airway clear with a suction machine, to emergency care if something went wrong with the ventilator, to helping him get settled in bed at night. "She was so amazing," Robertson said. "It was incredible to watch her, just about daily, have to figure out how to adjust to his loss of function. She was constantly trying to figure out how he could be as independent as possible until he absolutely could not be anymore."

Aiding Keith and Lynn in that quest was Sherry Odom, their physical therapist and friend. She made it her mission to help improve Keith's walking in the weeks after he was released from the hospital. She would come over determined to lead him around the house, but he would only want to walk from his bed to his chair, not from room to room. The effort was too taxing, and the ordeal with the vent had weakened him considerably. Even ECU baseball, with the postseason looming, had faded into the background that spring. But then one Monday in May the university announced that the Conference USA Baseball Tournament would be played at Grainger Stadium in Kinston, just thirty minutes from Greenville.

"Lynn called me and said, 'Keith says you need to push him harder, because he wants to go to Kinston, and he needs to be able to walk down those front steps.'" Odom said. "And I was like, 'I have been trying to push him, and he has not been cooperating.'" All Keith needed was the right motivation; the chance to watch his team in the postseason was all it took for him to submit to Sherry's therapy. "When I got over there, he walked all the way to the den."

To make Keith as comfortable as possible for the trip, Lynn took Mike Odom to a local furniture store to pick out a recliner for the van. Keith insisted that Mike go along, Sherry said, because he wanted a man's input. Once his friends had the chair, they proceeded to outfit a van belonging to Karen Sneed, a local woman who had volunteered to drive to the tournament. They took the middle seat out of the Sneeds' van and replaced it with the recliner, then loaded Keith in for the twenty-five-mile drive to Kinston. At that time, the Pirates were 37–18 and had drawn the sixth seed going into the double-elimination tournament. It was the team's first season in Conference USA, having moved over from the smaller Colonial Athletic Conference the previous fall.

Before the first pitch was thrown, Coach was positioned in his van with a good view of the action—adjacent to right field just outside the fence. What followed was a series of Pirate wins that surprised even the players, a classic case of a team peaking precisely at the right time. ECU defeated Texas Christian and South Florida and the University of Houston to win the C-USA title. Houston, the number one seed, had gone 41–14 that season and was highly favored to take the trophy. ECU, observed Eason, was David that day to Houston's Goliath.

The ECU assistants had planned their pitching rotation for the weekend to conclude on Sunday with Davy Penny, a young man from Benson, North Carolina, with a rocketing fastball. Eason believed that no other Pirate pitcher could have prevailed against Houston, and if ECU had lost one earlier game—and been forced to rise from the elimination bracket—then Penny would have been used earlier and wouldn't have been available that day. McMullan and Eason, true to their convictions, didn't use LeClair's presence to fire up the players, but everyone in that stadium felt the palpable influence of the coach in the silver van on the baseline.

"Every single time that Houston mounted any kind of rally, we'd have something spectacular happen," said volunteer assistant George Whitfield, who remembers one Cougar at-bat when they had runners on first and second and hit a hard line-drive to shortstop Luke Cherry, who turned an improbable double play with second baseman Jedd Sorenson. "And the last time it happened, I turned to Mac and I said, 'We've got a tenth player out there today. We were doing things that were unbelievable."

"I remember the looks on Coach Mac's and Coach Eason's faces," Bryant Ward said of the moment when the Pirate's victory was secured. "I don't know if it was relief or excitement. It was one of those deals where you look around and you see a lot of different emotions. You don't just see thirty-five guys excited because they won a conference championship. It felt like there was a lot more to it."

Third out, ninth inning, and the Pirates had prevailed. Davy Penny, the winning pitcher, ran over and grabbed a cooler full of Gatorade. Suddenly, in a display that would live on as an indelible image of triumph in the midst of trial, every Pirate player followed Penny to that parked van. As Lynn and Keith and friends sitting inside wept, the players poured the Gatorade over the front of the van, and then lined up one by one at the van door to congratulate their coach. The local newspaper captured Penny holding up a sign, his face etched with the emotional road map that had been his 2002 season. The poster board read, in bold black letters, "KEITH."

"Keith could put his foot out," said Sherry Odom, who was

inside the van that afternoon. "And to see him do high fives with his feet to all the players as they walked by his door—the tears were just everywhere—on the boys, and Keith and us. It was just incredible."

Back on campus with that improbable title under their belts, the ECU players waited for the Monday after Memorial Day, when the NCAA postseason baseball field is always announced on live television. As the Pirates were gathered in their clubhouse, five hours away Jack Leggett and his Clemson players were also glued to a television. The Tigers had one of their best teams in years, and a regional bid was a sure thing, but Leggett wondered if they would be a host school and who their visiting opponents might be. Every regional started with four teams, and the one survivor moved on to the Super Regional, which then led to Omaha.

The brackets started to appear on the screen. Clemson was a host city. The three teams that would come to play were Elon, Georgia Southern, and East Carolina. Suddenly Leggett had trouble thinking about pitching matchups or opponent records. He was in an emotional maelstrom over the visit of his friend and protégé. "When they got assigned to our regional, I went, 'Oh no,'" he said. "Because I wanted to see him, and I wanted to be with him, but I also wanted them to go to Omaha and I wanted us to go to Omaha."

In Greenville, Keith's core group of friends was planning their seven-hour trip to Clemson. Lynn's parents were driving separately, Joey Perry was piloting the van, the recliner was in place, and the Odoms brought their kids along for a vacation to scorching South Carolina. Traveling twenty-five miles to Kinston was one thing, Sherry Odom said, but that adventure was something else entirely. "I told Lynn, 'This is crazy,'" she said. "We're taking a man on a vent, in an unsecured chair, down the Interstate, following Lynn's mom, who was a wide-open driver. Keith was funny. I said, 'Keith, this is ridiculous.' And he said, 'If we get in a wreck and I die, so what?'"

The group arrived safely and was greeted by people from the Winchesters' church who would take care of all their meals for the duration of the tournament. It was a hot weekend, and the momentum that had carried the Pirates through the C-USA tournament was enough for the earlier games but not for their powerhouse host. The Pirates defeated Elon, then lost to Clemson, then beat Georgia Southern out of the losers' bracket. The regional final pitted them against Clemson again, and the home team dominated 21–1. In a career that spanned more than three decades, Leggett probably never enjoyed a victory less.

"Everything we did was right," Leggett said. "We score twenty runs or something, and I'm going, 'All I need is one more. I don't need fifteen.' It was tough. Because I knew that was probably the end of his coaching days. One of the toughest things I look back on is that I coached against Keith in his last game."

The Clemson players had heard all about Keith from their coach, about his character and his courage and his tenacity on the baseball field. After that regional final another line of players filed past the van door, but this time they were clad in a mixture of purple and orange. One by one, Tiger and Pirate players tapped Coach on the foot. Clemson would go on to defeat Arkansas in the Super Regional and make its ninth trip to Omaha, where the Tigers would lose in the semifinals to South Carolina. Leggett took it harder than usual, and every subsequent postseason became a quest to win a national championship, not just for his team, but for Keith.

A year earlier, ECU athletic director Mike Hamrick had assured Keith that he had the coaching job until he let the university know that he was no longer able to do the job. After the Clemson trip, the LeClairs asked Hamrick to come over, and Keith officially stepped down as the ECU head baseball coach. Hamrick accepted his resignation, but not completely. After a phone call to Chancellor Richard Eakin, Hamrick asked Keith to be his special assistant, allowing him

Neal Sears and Davy Penny pour Gatorade over the van Keith was sitting in to watch the Conference USA tournament in Kinston, N.C., in May 2002.

to continue with the same salary and health insurance.

Hamrick and others started visiting the LeClair home on a regular basis. Hamrick still sought his input on issues regarding baseball personnel and the stadium project. Friends tried to adjust to the changes they saw in his condition. Through that summer, communication became more of a challenge, as his feet became weaker and his ability to point to letters on the board became slower. By the fall of 2002 Keith was living in an almost-silent world. His mind hadn't diminished in the least, but his ability to express himself had nearly disappeared.

7
Team Keith

IN JUST A MATTER OF MONTHS, THE SETTING OF KEITH'S DAYS had made a dramatic shift from the baseball field to home. It would remain this way for four years. Restricted to a wheelchair and forced to silence by the rapid onset of his disease, Keith and his family entered a phase dominated by the medical procedures and terminology that had always felt like foreign territory before. But even if life became an endless series of housebound days, the LeClairs were far from lonely. For a family that had always valued their privacy, they quickly adapted to a revolving door of friends, medical professionals, and others from the community who just wanted to help in some way.

Some of those visitors were Christians who felt compelled to pray with Keith. Lynn remembers a day before Keith got the vent when he was struggling with an incessant cough and a group from a Greenville church knocked on the door. "Audrey opened up the door and she goes, 'Mom, it's strangers!' And I go to the door, and this lady's standing there, and she says, 'Hi, we're from First Pentecostal Holiness Church, and we brought you this chocolate peanut butter pie, and we came to pray with Coach LeClair.' And he's upstairs, and he's literally been coughing for two hours.'"

Keith didn't feel like he could come downstairs, so Lynn led the group of a dozen Pentecostals up the stairs, shoving laundry baskets in the closet ahead of them. The strangers prayed fervently over Keith, and he didn't cough once the rest of the night. "Constantly, it was like God showed up," Lynn said. "But the other part of it, with our kids, is that we had things very structured before. One of us washed dishes, one gave baths, then we did story, prayers, and bedtime. So all of a sudden, people are showing up here and there. I think for the kids it had to be a complete upheaval, because they didn't know exactly what was going on."

Many of those stopping by were current or former Pirate baseball players, whom Audrey and J.D. just considered a bunch of big brothers. But the mounting demands on their mother's time and their father's disability meant that Audrey—who turned eight the year her dad went on the ventilator—and five-year-old J.D. had to grow up a little faster than most kids their ages.

"I definitely became more independent," Audrey reflected. "We would have to go upstairs, and we would have to tuck ourselves in, and just know that Mom couldn't always be there. And I guess it made me stronger, too, and more sympathetic for others and what they're going through."

Before long, the LeClairs had ten hours a day of home health nursing care. A nurse would come in the early morning so that Lynn could get the kids to school, and would leave late in the afternoon. The nurses were invaluable when it came to helping care for Keith, but they brought their distinct problems and personalities into the home, too. The first nurse had a military demeanor, and she would spread out medical equipment on the table and order the kids not to touch anything, because it was sterile. Some became trusted family friends and experts at reading Keith's non-verbal cues.

Nurses and other visitors to the home found in Keith a free counselor—a willing listener whose opinion they found valuable. Being able to help others had the added benefit of giving Keith a sense of purpose. "I think maybe because he was walking the line between life and death, they thought he was holding more wisdom than some of their healthy friends," Lynn said. "They would all come in, and that was the thing to do, to come in and sit down and tell Keith what was going on."

As crowded as the LeClairs' den became at times, there were still people close to the family who were reluctant to visit. Clayton McCullough, who played his last inning for ECU at that Clemson Regional, was one of many young men who struggled with a mental tug of war during that time: They missed their coach and wanted to support him, but they were also scared of what new changes in him they might see. "I remembered him the way he was before, and it was hard to see him that way," McCullough said.

ECU groundskeeper Joey Perry found that he was feeling sorry for himself because he was so apprehensive about seeing his friend's deterioration. He had to check himself and call on his own Christian faith to bring him to the place he knew he needed to be: the LeClairs' door. "I've seen a lot of diseases in my family and around, and by far that's the worst thing I've ever seen put on a human being," Perry said. "At least in most of them your mind is gone, but when your mind is good and your body's done, and you can see other people's expressions, and you can see what it's doing to your family . . . I think God puts things on you that you can handle, and He must have known that Keith was a special guy, because I don't think I could handle that."

Matt Stillwell, a former Catamounts player who went from baseball player to country music singer, scheduled concerts for Eastern North Carolina as often as he could, with an ulterior motive. As limited as Keith was physically during that time, Stillwell still felt like he got better acquainted with him during those visits than he ever had through his WCU baseball career. "The true measure of a man is what he did after baseball," Stillwell said. "You don't know what kind of a man you are until you're faced with adversity like that."

October of 2002, just months after he officially stepped down as ECU's head baseball coach, Keith LeClair was inducted into the East Carolina Athletics Hall of Fame. Later that month he and Lynn are honored at a Pirates football game. At this point Keith was riding in a wheelchair that he could drive himself with hand controls.

As Keith's visitors found inspiration from him, Lynn toiled behind the scenes, trying to navigate one unpredictable day after another. The addition on the house and the home nursing care were helpful to her, but there were still days when the pressures of caring for Keith, raising the kids, and keeping up with the house seemed like a heavier load than she could bear. In one short period, friend Stuart Robertson said, the refrigerator leaked all over the new hardwood floors, and the washing machine, dishwasher, and stove all stopped working and had to be replaced. And then there were the times when the nurses called in and said they wouldn't be able to come that day.

"One time Keith was going around and around in circles in the middle of the living room in his wheelchair, and she couldn't stop it," Robertson said. "Another time when the nurse didn't show up, I opened the door and I could hear the ventilator beeping. Lynn was in there bagging Keith, and J.D. and Audrey were outside playing, and J.D. got hurt on his bicycle, and he's out there screaming bloody murder."

As the LeClairs coped with the home traffic, those close to Keith were doggedly investigating options that would again allow him to communicate with the people around him. It was Lynn, prompted by East Carolina head track coach Bill Carson, who first learned about something called an Eyegaze machine, which allowed users to type or synthesize speech just by looking at control keys on a monitor. A specialized video camera mounted below the screen constantly monitors one of the user's eyes, and those images interact with image processing software to determine where the user is looking on the screen. Lynn knew that the Eyegaze could be a lifeline for Keith, but it cost more than $15,000. To make the purchase possible, she turned to an account that was available for Keith's special needs. The money was raised by events at both East Carolina and Western Carolina, and even some from an auction in his hometown in New Hampshire. Even though part of that money had already gone to buy a special van fitted with a lift for Keith, there was still enough, with the help of insurance, to buy the Eyegaze. The machine arrived in early 2003. "What a wonderful day that was," Stuart Robertson said.

Everyone was excited about the possibilities the Eyegaze would open for Keith, but no one could have imagined the impact that one man, working through one piece of technology, could actually have. At first the LeClairs saw the Eyegaze strictly as a communication device, and before long Keith figured out how to type efficiently by using only his eyes. It may not have been his real voice, but he could talk again— ask visitors about baseball games, tell Lynn and the kids he loved them, remind J.D. not to run in the house. And then one day Keith discovered that his new machine had an even broader application when connected it to his computer. Nelson Cooper was visiting the day he realized that, with just eye movement, he could navigate the internet and write and receive e-mails.

"I will never forget how liberated he felt," Cooper said. "He said, 'I don't know why I haven't been doing this for months. It was like he had just made parole. He had gained back something. He gained back the ability to see some information if he wanted to, to communicate with friends by e-mail. And he felt so good. You could see it in his eyes."

"It just opened up his world," said Chuck Young, who witnessed Keith getting faster and faster at communicating via the Eyegaze. "He could buy Lynn a present without her knowing about it. He would have watched Chad Tracy in a Diamondbacks game on TV, and then he was e-mailing him. It was like it gave him purpose and worth."

The fact that computer technology became such a vital open door for Keith was truly ironic in light of his technological ignorance before his diagnosis, Dave Kemble noted. During his coaching days, he had a computer in his office, but he never turned it on. Everything he did in those days was handwritten. When he acquired his Eyegaze, Keith suddenly became one of the most plugged in people Kemble knew. It wasn't unusual for visitors to find him watching one game on television, listening to another on the radio and following dozens on the internet through Gametracker. Of special interest were the games of his former teams and the teams of his baseball friends. If one of his former players who went on to coach in Division I had a big game with his team, he was sure to hear from Keith afterwards.

For a year starting in September 2003, LeClair even wrote a baseball column for bonesville.net, an independent website devoted to East Carolina sports. LeClair's writings covered the world of baseball from college to the major leagues, and they displayed his intricate knowledge of the game. "After being sidelined with Lou Gehrig's disease the past two years, it feels great to be able to finally get online and talk baseball with fans," he wrote in a message attached to his first column. In his entry for May 2, 2004, Keith wrote a laudatory column about his predecessor, Gary Overton, and made a case for the former coach's election to the East Carolina Athletic Hall of Fame.

But no use of the Eyegaze computer had as widespread an impact as the Christian devotionals that Keith started writing and e-mailing to friends in 2003. He had continued the habit he started when he was diagnosed and was reading the Bible for extended periods of time, Young explained. Before long, he started to process what he was learning about God by writing it out. In February of 2004, Keith made an appearance at the fundraising banquet for Sportworks, Young's ministry to East Carolina athletes. While Keith stood at his side, Young read a devotional his friend had written about the familiar story of David versus Goliath. But Keith's point of view was to look at Goliath and to see himself in the mighty giant who was unexpectedly humbled that day. "It was from the perspective of Goliath thinking he was invincible," Young said. "I haven't heard a pastor or anybody else ever teach on that, so it was clearly an insight God gave him to his particular situation."

At first Keith only sent out the devotionals to a few people, but those recipients would forward the words on to others, and before long friends, acquaintances, and total strangers were writing to encourage Keith and to let him know how his insights had drawn them closer to God. Jim Toman was a colleague in coaching who had never even known Keith all that well, but when he connected with him through e-mail, their relationship deepened. Toman, who went on to become the head coach at Liberty University, was new to the Christian faith at that time, and he counts Keith as one of his greatest spiritual mentors.

For childhood friends like Brian Pickering, the Keith they saw coming through the devotionals was a man with a different dimension than the boy who had lived and breathed baseball. "The e-mails were so powerful," Pickering said. "He was very spiritual. I just remember thinking, 'You don't grow up expecting to learn so much from someone your age,' and here I am reading those e-mails saying, 'Here's a guy who's this sick, but still positive, still fighting, still has things in perspective, and still has hope.'"

"Here he had this disease that was taking his life, and he was growing stronger and stronger in his walk," added Carson, who attended a weekly coaches' Bible study led by Chuck Young at the LeClair home. "He probably was responsible in that year for reaching more people for the Lord in Greenville than all the ministers in that area put together."

Keith also saw an opportunity, with the help of the Eyegaze machine, to correct one regret he had harbored about his coaching years. He told Young that he knew he had worked hard to teach his players not only about baseball, but about honor, perseverance, leadership, and hard work. But as his own faith blossomed, he wished he had done more to point his players to Christ. So he enlisted Young's help in an ambitious endeavor—the purchase, embossing, and delivery of 150 purple leather Bibles, one for every young man who had played for him at ECU.

To further encourage the recipients, Keith wrote a devotional called "The Ten Finger Prayer." He and Chuck printed the writing on labels and affixed them to the inside cover of each Bible. In the devotional, LeClair shared several of his favorite verses, and encouraged each former Catamount and Pirate player to search his heart and examine his priorities. He wrote: "We are all going to face many trials and tribulations in life, and eventually we will have choices to make— either trust our Lord and Savior Jesus Christ or reject him and walk down our own paths."

If Keith's access to e-mail was creating an ever-widening circle of influence, his closest friends were tightening up to form an inner core that would often be the difference between despair and hope in those last years. It was a new kind of team for Keith, one populated by men and women of diverse ages and backgrounds, and one which, its members agree, could only have been put together by God's hand. "All of us in a mix, it was completely not manmade," Sherry Odom said. "It was completely odd."

Soon after Keith came home with the vent, friends like Odom realized that Lynn would need help at night, after the nurse had gone home, to prepare Keith for the night and get him securely into bed. And because she was a physical therapist and had Keith's complete trust, Sherry drove to the LeClairs' house every night for months to do those things herself. Her husband Mike's main role was to take care of their two children while Sherry was gone, but a couple of times he filled in if she was ill or had an important commitment. On one such evening, Mike and others were helping move Keith into bed when his knees gave out and he hit the floor. "Well, Keith," Sherry kidded him on her next visit, "I miss a night and they drop you."

But even though Sherry's family was supportive of the hours she spent assisting the LeClairs, as the months passed everyone agreed that she could use some back-up. That's when Team Keith started to form in earnest, as the LeClairs asked some of the ones they trusted the most if they would be willing to help out regularly during holes in the nursing care schedule.

There were the Coopers, who moved back to Greenville from South Carolina in 2003 and jumped right into the rotation. Jerry Greene, a truck driver and ECU's ultimate baseball fan, became the regular Monday night helper. Dave Kemble, the ECU manager who had been scared to see Keith sick just months before, was still in college when he was drafted for Team Keith on Sunday mornings and up to two nights a week. Chuck Young was a mainstay and the LeClair's personal minister. Rounding out the team were Stuart Robertson, Keith's former speech therapist whose bonds with the LeClairs quickly surpassed the professional, and Michelle Mazey, who came to Greenville when her ex-husband Randy took over as the ECU baseball coach but stayed for friendships like the ones she was making by serving Keith and Lynn.

Kemble was the youngest and initially the most reluctant team member, but early in their friendship, as Lynn observed him wash team uniforms on road trips, she had seen something special in him. She sought him out as one of her choices to help provide care to Keith, and he agreed despite his misgivings. He recalled the first time he went to the LeClairs' not just as a visitor, but as an official helper: "I was scared to death. Holy cow. We were sliding him on this sliding board from the wheelchair to the bed, and I almost thought I was going to drop him. You had to know your role. And it was funny, because you would work with different people. And if you were used to doing it one way, and they were used to doing it another, that made it a challenge."

The members of the inner circle became experts at reading the cues Keith could give with the only parts of his body that he could still move. Early on, Young set up a bell near Keith's toe, so that he could ring it in bed when he needed Lynn to suction his vent. When he couldn't move his toe anymore, they configured a buzzer that he could press with his thumb. And when you really needed to know what was going on with Keith, friends said, you only needed to check his eyes.

"I always knew his emergency eyes, when something was really wrong," Sherry Odom said. One night the Odoms were both there aiding with the bedtime routine when they accidentally knocked the vent cart over and shut off Keith's oxygen. "Keith normally gave me that emergency, 'My finger's caught' or 'You've got something wrong' look, but he didn't that night. He gave me that, 'What have they done now?' look."

Sometimes other commitments meant that team members arrived at nine or ten, close to bedtime, but Greene always got there by seven o'clock or so. That gave him time just to talk with Keith, and also ensured that they were always settled by eight, when hit sitcom *Everybody Loves Raymond* came on television. One Monday night when Greene had just started coming, he learned a vital lesson from Keith about the value of leaving his agenda at the LeClairs' door and just focusing on his friend. "I glanced at my watch one night while I was there," Greene said. "And he said, 'You've got somewhere you have to be?' I said, 'Absolutely not. I'm right where I want to be.' And from that day on I never wore a watch to his house again."

With the help of his Eyegaze machine, Keith loved to talk for hours to his friends who visited—about baseball, politics, family, or other things that were happening in their lives. What he didn't enjoy about evenings was the inevitable approach of bedtime. He would do anything he could to put it off, Sherry Odom said, because he had so much trouble getting comfortable in bed, and once settled, he and Lynn rarely slept soundly. "You almost felt a little guilty when you finished up at night and left at eleven, knowing he could not get comfortable," Mike Odom said. Sherry remembers waking up in the wee hours and wondering if Keith and Lynn were okay. She remembers thanking God that if she had a wrinkled sheet under her shoulder, she could easily smooth it out.

As they completed so many necessary tasks, Team Keith also became a vital source of hope for the LeClairs. They prayed fervently and frequently for Keith, and they continued to believe with the LeClairs that healing was possible. Robertson left their house many nights in tears, praying for the miracle that she ardently believed could come to pass.

The LeClairs' core team, Keith's former players, and other friends weren't just witness to the family's steadfast faith and courage in the face of a ravaging disease. They were also participants in the lighter side of life in that house—Keith's unbounded sense of humor that shone through even when he had only his eyes to bring levity to his situation. "So many times when I went down there, everyone would be gathered around the computer," said Kevin LeClair, who made the trip from up north as often as he could during those years. "He was always joking around. Whoever came over, he would type out something sarcastic or funny, and you would see his eyes kind of look up, and then get back on his thought."

Because he couldn't eat solid food, Keith's nutrition came through a tube inserted in his stomach. A nutritional supplement called Boost was frequently on the "menu." One day he invited ECU pitcher Davy Penny, whom he had coached for three seasons, to come over and watch a football game. At the time, Penny's jaw was wired shut because of an injury from a wayward ball. Stuart Robertson was there when he made the plans with Penny: "Keith asked him, 'Are you going to watch the game Monday night? Well, come on over and we'll knock back a couple of cans of Boost."

Link Jarrett didn't get to meet Keith until late in his illness, when Jarrett was hired as an ECU assistant coach in 2005. But LeClair remembered Jarrett as the former Florida State shortshop who had hit a crucial home run in Western Carolina's agonizing NCAA Regional loss thirteen years earlier, in 1992. "I walked in to his house that day and he wrote on his screen, 'After hitting that home run, I shouldn't even let you in my house,'" Jarrett said.

Brian Chandler, Keith's old Walpole friend who had settled in nearby Raleigh, came to visit every few months, and he and Keith laughed and reminisced about the things they did growing up in Walpole. Chandler was comforted, during those conversations, when he realized that Keith's quick wit was very much intact. "You knew right off when you went to visit him that he was still the same Keith, regardless of what the disease was doing to him physically," he said. First-time visitors, especially, recalled that Keith joked around with them right when they walked in, and many could tell that he was using humor to diffuse any nervousness or tension that person might feel about witnessing his disabilities.

One of Keith's personal heroes—and the most noteworthy visitor to pass through the LeClair home—came in February of 2005. Cal Ripken, Jr., was in Greenville to speak to a group, and Kirk Dominick, a local man who knew Ripken, asked Ripken's agent if the baseball great's schedule might have an opening for a few minutes with Keith. Originally, a brief stay was all Ripken could manage—Keith was told that he was coming on a Saturday afternoon but could only spare fifteen minutes. He was late, and Keith started worrying that he wasn't coming at all. But when Ripken finally arrived, he didn't seem like a man in a hurry.

"I expected the old, 'Hello I'm Cal Ripken, and it's nice to meet you' deal, and then, *Adios, amigo,*" LeClair wrote in one of his devotionals in May 2005. "You know, the big time welcome where you blow in and blow out. Well, that was the farthest thing from the truth when he arrived. Cal Ripken, Jr., was the most humble and grounded person I have ever met. He spent more than an hour with Lynn, Audrey, J.D. and I, just talking baseball and family. If you didn't know his name, you would have never guessed that you were carrying on a conversation with a Hall of Famer. "

Dominick made the visit to the LeClair home with Ripken, and he said that the two had an immediate bond, and both were in tears at one point. "You could really just see this mutual admiration," Dominick said. "I still get chills thinking about it."

When the hordes of visitors thinned out, it was Team Keith that remained and lovingly helped with Keith's care. And when the nurses had clocked out and the team had returned to their own families, it was Keith's truest inner circle—Lynn, Audrey, and J.D.—who found strength they didn't know they had to weather seismic change and soak up every bit of quality time with Keith that was available to them.

Some of Audrey's favorite memories of her dad came from talking with him through the computer. He would call her his pet name, "Pookie Pookie," and ask her about school or discuss the shows they loved to watch together, like *American Idol*. "He always picked the winner," she added. "I don't know how." When they watched the Kentucky Derby together, they would each pick a horse. When they watched baseball, Yankees-fan Audrey would give her dad grief about his favorite team, the Red Sox. Sometimes, before Keith settled into bed, he would leave messages for Audrey and her brother on the computer for them to read the next morning.

J.D. was too small to understand much of what was happening—he was only five when Keith went on the vent—but he recalls playing a tic-tac-toe game with his dad on the computer and the times they would all go to church together with Keith in the wheelchair. ECU baseball alumni and other friends were always willing to go outside and play ball with J.D., and Keith loved to watch them play catch. Even years later, J.D. remembered the sound of the computer voice that his dad would use to tell him not to talk back to his mother and to tell him that he loved him, every night before bed. "It was kind of weird and robotic, but at least I got to talk to him," he said.

Finally, when the house was quiet and dark and Keith had a persistent itch or a need for medicine or suction, it was Lynn who was his steadfast hero. To Jerry Greene, she was an angel. Keith's former assistant Kevin McMullan said that she had "a master toolbox," a store of everything she needed to deal with the crisis before her. For many of the young people who frequented the LeClairs' house, she provided an example of unwavering devotion in marriage that they would someday take with them to the altar.

"She was a spectacularly patient and caring and giving person through this whole thing," said Jack Leggett. "She had to do things that were really difficult, and I never heard her complain one time. It was something to watch. He married the right girl."

The LeClair family on March 4, 2005, at a ceremony honoring East Carolina's first game in its new baseball stadium, named Clark-LeClair stadium after Keith and donor Bill Clark.

8

Home

FOR MORE THAN THREE YEARS KEITH WAS MOSTLY HOUSE-bound, immobile and unable to eat, talk, or breathe on his own. But he had stayed remarkably upbeat through that time, cracking jokes and spending more time asking about visiting friends and their lives than dwelling on his own. Early on, doctors had given him a prescription for the antidepressant Zoloft, citing the connection between debilitating illness and depression. But his spirits stayed so high that he never seemed to need anything like that. It was only toward the end of 2005 that friends noticed a shift in his demeanor, when his lifeline to the outside world started to fail him.

One of Keith's emotional anchors was certainly his steadfast faith, and another was his ability to stay connected to his world through his Eyegaze computer. It was only when he started to lose the Eyegaze that he gave quarter to a measure of frustration and despair. Just as every other muscle had succumbed to the paralysis wrought by ALS, his eye strength would eventually go as well, his inner circle knew. At times they even wanted to cut him off from his computer screen, just so he could rest his eyes and maybe gain a few more days of precious communication.

They tried eye drops and special cream, and an optometrist friend even put plugs in Keith's tear ducts to increase his eyes' ability to produce moisture. But his once-blazing speed forming sentences on the Eyegaze was diminishing rapidly. In November 2005 Nick Schnabel, a former player who was then an assistant baseball coach at West Point, was visiting the area for Thanksgiving and came by to see Keith. It was the last conversation Keith had with anyone using the computer. "He was struggling with it," Lynn said. "The muscles were weaker, and he couldn't blink. His eyes weren't shutting completely at night, so we were trying to tape them shut because he was getting ulcers on his eyes."

In upstate New York Tim Sinicki was in the midst of a typical off-season as the head baseball coach at Binghamton University. A college friend and teammate of Keith's at Western Carolina, Sinicki had incorporated e-mail communication with his old friend into his daily routine. He checked his in box regularly for personal notes or devotions from Keith, and after he read them, he often wrote a note back. One day that fall, Sinicki got an e-mail from Lynn instead, a heart-rending message that she sent to dozens of people. Keith had lost his ability to e-mail anyone, Sinicki read; he would not be hearing from Keith again.

After becoming comfortable with the technology that allowed them to talk back and forth with Keith, his friends found themselves reliving the frustration they felt before the Eyegaze came along. But he was much weaker this time around, and when they gave him his old alphabet board he struggled to point at the letters with any accuracy, and any messages he could get across were painstakingly slow. "That was terrible," Kemble said. "His ability to blink and say yes was slowly going. That very, very small twitch, motor neurons, he was starting to lose those. He tried that board again, and it didn't work. If he didn't have that [Eyegaze] technology, there's no way he would have wanted to live that long."

And it wasn't just his eyes. Keith had deteriorated in every way, Lynn said, with each daily task becoming a daunting chore involving tubes, monitors, lifts, and other machines. ALS is a ruthless thief that robs just about everything from its victims, and Keith had been ravaged by it. "If you can be hooked up to anything, he was hooked up to it," she said. "More and more, there was a feeling of entrapment in his own body."

Lynn made an appointment with a nurse who worked for the Eyegaze company, and she visited to examine Keith and the technology. Her report was discouraging. There was nothing further they could do to keep Keith connected. He was being kept alive with the help of the vent, and his intention for years had been to make the most of the time he could grab, to soak up Lynn and the kids and share the hope of his faith with as many people as he was allowed to reach. His strong eyes had been the window to that world of love and purpose, and when his eyes failed it seemed Keith was slipping away, too. "Keith settled that he was ready to die," Lynn said.

For years Keith and Lynn had wondered, talked, and prayed about the end and what it would be like. Their closest friends, like Sherry Odom, had hoped that something natural, like a blood clot, would take any decision out of the LeClairs' hands. To guide them, Lynn had been talking to a family friend in Vermont whose daughter had been stricken by ALS. She told the LeClairs that the family had gathered around her daughter's bed, said their goodbyes, and turned off the vent. "I couldn't imagine it at the time," Lynn remembered.

Lynn had plumbed her own depths and emerged with an inner strength she hadn't dreamed she possessed. Even her mother had marveled at how her daughter could function with almost no sleep, a former grade-school teacher performing around-the-clock nursing duties while keeping up a home and taking care of the needs of two young children. She was drawing energy from the Lord and her love for Keith, and she truly felt that she could take care of him for as long as she was called to do so. But there was one thing she simply couldn't do for him, and she knew it. "I told him, 'I can take care of you, but I cannot shut a vent off.'"

They turned to their faithful friend Chuck Young, whom they considered their personal minister. For the LeClairs, Young had been everything from pastor to technical advisor when the computer acted up, to inventor, scouring stores for items that he could put together to help keep Keith comfortable when he developed new aches or sores. Chuck had been one of the few who would help with anything Keith needed done, and much of that time in the LeClair home those four years ran together in his mind. But his memory is crystalline when it comes to the phone call he received one day in the fall of 2005. He was on the East Carolina football field, talking to new head coach Skip Holtz about his ministry to the Pirate football players, when his cell phone rang. It was the LeClairs' attorney, asking him to assume Keith's power of attorney and to make the final decision about when the end of his life had come.

As it turned out, the family attorney never completed the process passing the responsibility to Young, but the request proved their implicit trust in Young. Even without the legal designation, he sought to guide the LeClairs with humility and complete deference to them. He saw his role as that of a counselor, helping them process their tangled emotions and channel every concern back to the spiritual reality, even though his deep love for his friend kept his own emotions at the surface.

"There were several elements," Young said. "I was pushing him, saying, 'God's using you,' because I certainly didn't want to see him stop. There were times for Lynn and Keith when he would say, 'Man, this is so hard. I'm ready to stop.' There was a time when Keith was ready and she wasn't. I don't know how many times he would say, 'I can't believe I'm sitting here planning my death.' Death is the one thing we weren't created for. It certainly isn't something where you think you have to pick a day and a time."

Keith was increasingly ready to stop fighting, certain that heaven and the Jesus he had fallen in love with were waiting for him when he died. With whatever communication he could muster, he and Lynn discussed it and settled on February 8, 2006, as the day the vent would be shut off. But as that day got closer, Lynn was completely unsettled, and she told Keith that she and the kids just weren't ready. "I just didn't feel like I had time to prepare the kids," she said. "I didn't have time for anything. I asked for a little more time."

Keith's team of caregivers and friends were torn, too, because while it was hard to see him forced back into silence, the alternative seemed harder still. "That January and February, after he lost the ability to communicate, I came home one night, and I was just like, 'I just need somebody to help me comprehend. I never dreamed the Lord would allow it to get that far,'" Sherry Odom said. After Keith died, she told Lynn, "I don't know how the Lord could have allowed it to get to that point. And she said, 'It was because of me. I wasn't ready to let him go.'"

The LeClairs went about the impossible task of choosing a new date, even as milestones came and went—like Keith's fortieth birthday on February 28. Around that time, Western Carolina contacted them. Keith's former WCU teammate Todd Raleigh, who had followed him as the Catamounts head coach, had pressured the athletic department to do something unprecedented—retire a WCU player's baseball jersey. WCU leaders agreed and hastily selected April 11, 2006, as the date for the ceremony. It wasn't the first baseball honor Keith had received—in the fall of 2002 he was inducted into the athletic halls of fame of both Western Carolina and East Carolina Universities. The ceremonies, on both sides of the state, drew hordes of friends and supporters. But the retirement of a number was something exceedingly rare in college baseball, so rare that Keith would be the first player at Western to be so honored. That spring, Keith and a group of friends and family got into the van for his last trip to his alma mater.

The day, and the ceremony, reminded those assembled of the Hall of Fame induction four years earlier, but the major difference was Keith's condition. Keith was able to get out of the van briefly, bundled up against a brisk mountain wind, but everybody who wanted to visit him had to do so in the van. "We thought he would still be able to communicate, but he couldn't," said WCU administrator Steve White. He wasn't well enough to watch the game that followed the ceremony, between WCU and Clemson.

Dr. Scott Higgins, a member of the WCU faculty and a close friend of Keith's during his years there, received a warm greeting from him at the Hall of Fame induction. When he went to the van to see him for the jersey retirement, however, Keith could no longer communicate to his friend that he recognized him. Another former Western professor, Jim Hamilton, only remembers the bittersweet nature of the evening. "It was, as you can imagine, not a happy time for me, but I wouldn't have been anywhere else."

The Catamounts radio network devoted its entire pregame show that day to memories and stories about Keith. During the pregame jersey retirement ceremony, Jack Leggett and Todd Raleigh both spoke, and Chuck Young read a statement from Keith. The speakers that night were characterized by their tears.

"He has everything I want my players to have," said Raleigh, who went on to become the head coach at the University of Tennessee. "He has everything I want my son to have. Courage. Integrity. The work ethic. The competitiveness. The ultimate team player and the ultimate team coach."

"Great people are never forgotten," Leggett said. "People who make a tremendous impression on your life are never forgotten. And, even though we learned a lot of baseball from Keith, that pales in comparison to what we have learned

On April 11, 2006, Western Carolina retired the first baseball jersey in the program's history—the number 23 worn by LeClair. As part of the ceremony that day, Catamount players form an arch to welcome Keith, Lynn, Audrey, and J.D. into the stadium.

about ourselves and learned about life."

At the conclusion of the ceremony, a drape was pulled off of the stadium's back wall to reveal a large painted purple replica of LeClair's jersey with his number 23, which will never be worn again at Western Carolina. "I pray that in the years to come, when people see this 23, they will not think of an individual, but of a team of unity," LeClair said in the statement read by Young. "Without the support of others, none of this would have been possible."

It had taken Keith an hour to prepare even that simple message, as the only way he could communicate by then was to have someone go through the alphabet with him, one letter at a time, and look for the slightest movement in his eyes indicating "yes." Letter by painstaking letter, the message was formed.

Dozens of Keith's former players were in attendance at WCU, and the ones who couldn't make it were aware that something momentous was going on that day in the Blue Ridge Mountains. Jason Beverlin was playing baseball in Japan at the time, but he found the whole ceremony streamed on the internet, and he listened to every word from across the world.

Clemson, with Leggett at the helm, beat Western that day 8–3. For Leggett, it was one emotional day in a season that was rife with them. Every year since the Regional that pitted mentor against apprentice, Leggett had set his sights on a College World Series bid so that he could go to Omaha for Keith. In 2005, the Tigers had been one step away, at the Super Regional against Baylor University. His team won the first game, and then fell in the next two to end their season. In his Waco, Texas, hotel room the morning of the second game, his first call was to Keith.

"I was all choked up," he said. "I was a mess. Because I wanted so badly to take that team to Omaha. Physically, mentally, I was drained. I was carrying around the thought of us going to Omaha together, bringing him back some dirt from Omaha."

But 2006 was Clemson's year, and the Tigers qualified for the College World Series in Omaha. His team lost in the second round, but finally, just a month before he would say his final goodbye, Leggett had fulfilled his mission. And even if he couldn't talk to Keith on the phone anymore, everything about that trip to Nebraska was imbued with Keith's spirit.

Back in Greenville, spring was coming and the warm weather prompted Keith to request two final trips to places he loved: the beach and the mountains where Lynn's family lived. After the kids got out of school in June, they traveled to Atlantic Beach, staying in a ground-floor room in a

At Keith's request, the LeClair family took one last trip to the beach in June 2006 (Keith's vent can be clearly seen).

beachfront hotel so that Keith could get near the ocean. Then in early July, they loaded up the van again, with a nurse and a few friends, and headed to the South Carolina mountains. On the Fourth of July, they took two cars to watch the fireworks over nearby Lake Keowee, but that night stands out to Lynn for another reason.

The nurse and the others were in one car, and Lynn was in the van with only Keith and her father. Suddenly, as they were heading back to the house, the battery on the portable vent started to go, and Lynn was forced to keep Keith alive in the dark, on a rural road, with a manual bag valve mask that she attached to his face and then pumped by hand. "Dad pulled over, and I bagged him all the way home until we could get more light and take care of the vent." She couldn't conceive of Keith's life ending because of a dead battery. "I was just like, 'No, not like this. Not like this.'"

Amid travel plans and moments together that grew more precious, the LeClairs were still trying to pick a date. It got very frustrating for Young, he said, because they had to abandon a few days because people who needed to be present had conflicts. They also were careful to avoid dates with other significance, like Keith and Lynn's anniversary on June 22 (they celebrated fifteen years of marriage that summer). Finally, it was settled to turn off the vent on Monday, July 17, 2006.

The last use of the Eyegaze had been in November. "From January to July of 2006, we watched the continued deterioration of Keith's eyes," Lynn said. "We were given windows of opportunity for communication, but those opportunities became less frequent with passing days. Many times the muscles in his eyes would freeze, cutting conversations short. To save his eyes, we all became adept at completing words and sentences when possible." Fortunately, long before he had reached that stage he had discussed the situation with trusted friends and made his wishes known to Lynn.

For the LeClairs' regular visitors and the family, everything about those final weeks seems to be painted in bold strokes. As the day got closer, the kids started sleeping downstairs in their parents' room, to stay close. Team LeClair continued more or less on its schedule, but with a terrible sense of finality. On Stuart Robertson's last night sitting with Keith, she was nearly overcome with sadness and with the frustration that came from not understanding him anymore. "I was begging him, 'Please forgive me, because I don't know what you're trying to tell me. He just couldn't move his eyes at all.'" Robertson had kept up with the latest ALS research, and at one point near the end she told Keith that a breakthrough could be just around the corner. "I would tell him, 'In the next year or two, there's no telling what might be developed.' And he was like, 'Nope.' He was done."

Young was around most of the time in those final days, and he spent hours talking to Keith about the hope of heaven and the goodness of God. He also sought to assure both Keith and Lynn that they were free to make this decision without guilt. Keith knew that God was sovereign, but he struggled with the idea that they could be in control by voluntarily ending his life.

Young told him, "You're not taking your life. You're going to turn off the vent, and if God wants you to breathe you're going to continue to breathe." Later, Young explained, "We tend not to long enough for the Lord's return. We enjoy what's here. And we were still praying for healing, but at the same time knowing there was a great place he was headed to. It became an everyday conversation with him that this is what we long for. You're not going from the real world to a dream world. You're going from a temporary home to a permanent one."

One irony of Keith's final weeks is that many of the most vivid memories were centered around food. After all, Keith had not been able to eat solid food for more than four years. But he had always loved to eat, and somehow he managed to develop a fascination for cooking and food at the very time when he was unable to enjoy it. The Food Network was second only to baseball in his viewing preferences, and he often gave Lynn elaborate menus and asked her to make them for visitors.

"He would want me to bring in the plate so that he could see it," Stuart Robertson said. "And I would say, 'Keith, are you sure you really want to?' And he would say, 'No. I enjoy looking at it. I enjoy talking about it. I enjoy thinking about it. I just can't have it.'" Keith especially loved his mother's cooking, so when she came down to visit, he had specific culinary requests for her as well. But during that last weekend, Keith seemed to know that those closest to him would be too overwhelmed to think about food. So he took care of those arrangements himself.

The house was full of family and friends that weekend, and Keith managed to communicate that he wanted everyone to have pizza. But he didn't want the chain-restaurant pizza they usually ordered when they were feeding a group. He specifically requested that his guests eat pizza from Boli's, an independently-owned Greenville restaurant. Boli's was more expensive, but Keith was insistent. He had been listening to the radio for hours at a time during those days, since his eyes were too weak for the computer or the television. He had heard someone on the local station say that Boli's is consistently voted as the best pizza in Greenville. That night, he wanted his loved ones to have the best.

But that wasn't the last meal he arranged. One of his final nurses, Patricia Gibbs, also had a burgeoning catering business. Quietly, he arranged a menu with Patricia, asking her to cook a medley of ribs, Southern vegetables, cornbread, and other favorites of his. He asked her to have the feast ready on Monday afternoon, so that his friends and family could enjoy it together after he was gone. "His last thoughts were of taking care of everybody else," Robertson observed.

Dave Kemble had always gone to the LeClairs' on Sundays, to help Lynn while she got everyone ready for church. The routine had been dismantled by July 16, but nothing was going to keep Kemble away. He had served LeClair eloquently with his actions for years, but that day he found himself without the right words. "It was the last time I was going to see him and talk to him," he said. "And you want to say something clever, but words just can't describe what you want to say to the man who's meant so much to you."

Throughout that last day, Audrey rarely left her dad's bedside. She was almost twelve and keenly aware of everything that was happening, and she made no effort to hide her sadness. "Audrey cried her little heart out," Lynn said. "She knew more than J.D. about what was happening. J.D. would just kind of come into the room and go out and then come into the room and go out. But Audrey was just like right there. She just cried and cried and cried."

Patricia came in to help Keith get bathed and shaved that

day, and Lynn spent a lot of time trying to understand a word that he was trying to speak to her. She confirmed that it started with a "P," but the rest was just guesswork, and Keith kept indicating that she was wrong. Keith was trying hard to make his point, but even those who were usually the most skillful at understanding him were struggling.

That Sunday morning at Oakmont Baptist Church, which had been Keith's church home for nine years, youth minister Amy Andrews preached a sermon about a woman who had been hemorrhaging for decades and received healing just by touching the tassels on Jesus' robe as he passed by. As the parishioners left the service, they each received a small tassel as a reminder of the powerful healing available in Christ. The LeClairs didn't attend church that morning, but the Odoms did, and later that day Sherry grabbed her tassel and drove over.

"I went up to Keith and kissed him on the cheek and told him what the sermon was. I told him, 'Reach out for that tassel,'" she said.

On Monday, a small group including Chuck, Dr. Rick Figler, Oakmont Baptist pastor Dr. Greg Rogers, and a doctor from the local hospice joined Lynn, the kids, and Keith's and Lynn's parents at their home. Lynn put the tassel from Sherry in Keith's hand, and the hospice doctor simply switched off the vent. At the age of forty, Keith's battle with ALS was over.

"I stayed out of work that morning because I was just waiting for the phone call," Sherry Odom said. "When Chuck called me, I literally wanted to jump for joy because I was so thrilled that he wasn't trapped anymore. I have never been so emotionally conflicted in my life."

Keith blessed all who knew him with four additional years when he agreed to prolong his life by going on the ventilator. "It was never his intent to be kept alive by artificial means, but sometimes God has a different plan," Lynn recalled.

All over the country, from Walpole to Florida and California where former LeClair players were coaching, phones started buzzing as friends gulped and prepared to share the news that no one wanted to say out loud. Ex-WCU teammate Keith Shumate had woken up virtually every morning for three years with a singular thought: Would this be the day?

The LeClairs had taken care to ensure that Keith's death date didn't conflict with any milestones, but there was one they had missed. Jerry Greene had been over to see his friend every night the week before he died, and he came back to see Lynn on the day after. He pulled her aside and told her that Monday, July 17, had been his birthday.

"Why are you crying?" he asked, puzzled by Lynn's response. He then finished the rest of what he wanted to tell her. "Now every time I have a birthday I will realize that Keith met his Maker on the day I was born. And it will always be a wonderful, honoring memory."

The night of her husband's death, Lynn went to bed fatigued by grief and with her mind racing. Among other things, she was still wondering about that word that Keith was trying so emphatically to get across, the one that started with "P." She drifted off to sleep, then woke up at 3:23 in the morning—the first of many incidents involving Keith's number 23 that have seemed to follow those closest to him. And in those wee hours, she thought of Audrey and her deep sadness, and she heard in her spirit Keith's nickname for his beloved daughter.

"I woke up, and all of a sudden it just hit me," she said. "He wanted to say, 'Pookie Pookie.' I was telling him, 'OK, OK, I've got it. I've got it. You love her. I know you love her.' I know that's what it was, because she was so upset. And he was trying to say something to her." For the first night in years, Keith wasn't there next to her, but they managed to make a connection even after he was gone.

9
Celebration

THE FIGHT THAT HAD FOR YEARS DEFINED LYNN'S LIFE AND dictated the schedules of Keith's inner circle was finally over, and the days immediately following his death were marked by extreme emotions—sadness, relief, grief, joy, and, at times, pure exhaustion. Chuck Young became the official media spokesman for the family, and newspapers throughout the Southeast ran stories summarizing Keith's accomplishments on the field and his courage off of it.

The immediate task for Keith's closest friends was to plan the details of the funeral, and Young came to the process armed with specific requests from Keith himself. In the rare moments when he allowed himself to dwell on his grim diagnosis, he had discussed funeral observances with Chuck, and he was clear about a few central themes that should dominate any ceremony.

The first focus, Keith told his friend and spiritual mentor, was the truth of the Christian faith to which he had devoted his days and on which he pinned his hope for the afterlife. It was Keith's greatest desire that his funeral feature a clear proclamation of the gospel—Jesus' death on the cross for everyone, and each person's freedom to receive that gift and commit to a lifetime of following Christ. He fervently hoped that as people came to pay their respects to him, they might meet the Lord who had given him such passion and purpose.

The second theme Keith emphasized in those talks with

Chuck was his desire to honor Lynn. He wanted the service to be a tribute to her selflessness and pure love, and he even selected a song he hoped would be played in his wife's honor. He also requested that the program for the funeral be printed with the Biblical passage from Proverbs 31 that begins, "A wife of noble character who can find? She is worth far more than rubies."

Through a blur of a week, friends and former players trickled into Greenville in preparation for Friday, a day to be filled with two different services for Keith. The first would be a traditional closed-casket funeral at Oakmont Baptist Church in the middle of that afternoon, followed by an early-evening "Celebration of Life" at ECU's new baseball venue. The church funeral was planned out with four main speakers and a selection of music that was special to the LeClairs. For the stadium service, any former players or colleagues who wished to speak would have access to an open microphone on the field.

But before either of those services, the first observance was the visitation, set for Thursday night at Wilkerson's Funeral Home in Greenville. Mike and Sherry Odom were given the task of collecting remembrances from Keith's life to decorate the funeral home, and they gathered pictures and items from ECU, the LeClair home, and other friends. Western Carolina teammate Tim Sinicki, though from upstate New York, happened to be vacationing in Myrtle Beach. So Sinicki came through for the visitation, and he was overwhelmed by the visual reminders of his friend's legacy to baseball and beyond.

"I really enjoyed the opportunity not just to see his family, but the collection of photos and awards," Sinicki said. "It took you back to all of the times, chronicled his life in pictures, and gave you closure. You couldn't actually say goodbye to him when he was alive, but at that point I think it was very helpful to everyone because there were so many memories in the funeral home."

Friday morning dawned clear and hot, and Oakmont's spacious sanctuary filled up well before 2:00 P.M. The service opened with Oakmont members singing two songs that served as poignant reminders of Keith's transition from earth to a heavenly home: "Knowing You" and "When I Get Where I'm Going." The latter said, in part, "When I get where I'm going / there'll be only happy tears. / I will shed the sins and struggles / I have carried all these years. / And I'll leave my heart wide open / I will love and have no fear. / Yeah when I get where I'm going / don't cry for me down here."

After the songs, the mourners watched a video tribute to Keith, put together by ECU employees and set to the song "Who Am I" by Casting Crowns. The video combined pictures of Keith, career highlights, and quotes from public statements he made through the years of his illness. In one, Keith said, "If I can bring hope to one person through this disease, it will be worth all the pain and suffering my family and I have gone through."

The first speaker on the program was Chuck Young, who probably had more spiritual conversations with Keith than anyone else. He opened by clearly outlining the reason for Keith's hope even on his darkest days. "The reason this is a celebration is not because he was just such a good guy, and we don't celebrate because he did more good things than bad things, and we don't celebrate because he suffered, which he did," Young said. "He was a good guy and all that is true. But we celebrate because of Jesus. That's the only reason we can celebrate, because he trusted Jesus."

Young laid out two personal challenges for his listeners. First, he dared them to take the time to get to know Jesus Christ the way Keith had. The second task he presented was based on the Old Testament story of Joshua. Joshua was charged by God to lead the Israelites into the Promised Land, even though Moses, who had brought them to the edge of the land and poured his heart into the journey, was dead. Keith was teaching until his last breath, Young said, and he was a mentor to most of the people in the room. So like Joshua, those who knew Keith had a God-given task.

"As I look around the room, there are a whole lot of Joshuas out there that Keith put time into," he said. "And now it's your turn. Time to go out and to continue to take this thing a few innings more, and you're going to recruit some new guys, and you're going to train some new guys, and you're going to need to be growing yourself along the way."

In a statement released by Clemson just after Keith's death, Jack Leggett said Keith was "like a son, a brother, and a best friend to me." As he walked to the podium to address the church that day, Leggett's emotion was apparent, and he spoke many of his words directly to Lynn. He acknowledged her countless sacrifices over the five years of Keith's illness and said that they amounted to a priceless gift for the friends who loved him.

"Your patience, your life, your unselfishness, your kindness, your understanding, allowed J.D. and Audrey a chance to better know their father for a longer period of time," Leggett said as he looked down from the platform to Lynn in her front-row seat. "You gave Keith a chance to realize that he chose an unbelievably kind and patient woman as a wife. You gave us a chance to know you better, and to love and respect you for treating our friend with dignity, patience, and a level of love that we all will never forget."

Just a month earlier, as his team played in Omaha for college baseball's greatest prize, Leggett had frequently rubbed the number 23 he inscribed under the bill of his ball cap. But the ultimate symbol of Keith's legacy came when Leggett's Clemson players—who had never met Keith nor knew anything about him beyond what they learned from their coach—wrote "23" on their cleats.

"Not often in a lifetime does a person come along who

affects so many people so deeply," said Leggett, who also read a poem he wrote for Keith entitled "The Toughest Man I Know." "He'll make us all more thoughtful, more compassionate, tougher, more competitive, more caring, and more loving. We'll be passing on Keith's teachings forever, from generation to generation, and that's the mark of a great man."

The next speaker, representing Keith's bond with ECU baseball, was George Whitfield, the veteran coach Keith had hired for free nine years earlier. Whitfield recalled the story of the day Keith recruited him to the Pirates staff, and he also told some baseball stories that recalled Keith's steadfast leadership and ideals on the field. But some of Whitfield's greatest memories, he said, were in the back of the bus on dark road trips, when Keith would come and sit with him for a stretch.

"Keith would find his way back to my seat, and you know in all those five years we never talked about baseball coming home from a game," Whitfield said. "We talked about his family. He asked me about my children. He was very inquisitive about lots of different things, not only about baseball but about life."

They were three of the most important people in Keith's life, and Young, Leggett, and Whitfield each conveyed moving, heartfelt messages about the abiding value of his forty years. But the most poignant moment of the Oakmont Baptist service came not from a friend but from Keith himself. When Whitfield finished, Oakmont member Jeff Foster came forward to sing, "I Can Only Imagine" by Mercy Me, a song that imagines the wonder of a Christian meeting his Savior in heaven. Then senior pastor Greg Rogers came up, read several passages from the Bible, and recalled a visit he had with Keith in his office one day in August of 2001.

Keith had come for spiritual encouragement in light of the diagnosis he was, at that point, still trying to wrap his mind around. They talked for two hours, Rogers said, and Keith assured him that his faith was only growing as he took each step into this dark valley. At the time, Keith was part of a men's group at Oakmont that was studying *Experiencing God*, a book by Henry Blackaby centered on the theme that "God is always at work around you." Rogers felt that sitting across from him was a living example of that idea, and he spontaneously asked Keith if he would speak about his journey at church the following Sunday.

With that introduction, at the gathering called to mourn and honor Keith, Rogers directed the crowd to the screen, and suddenly a thirty-five-year-old LeClair appeared, mobile and fluid of speech, giving his testimony on a recording of that service on August 19, 2001. He told about his ascendancy in the baseball world but of his recent realization that he had not given up control to the Lord during those years. He remembered his shame before God, but he said that he found healing and forgiveness by diving into the words of the Bible.

"I'm just here to say, I hope you don't make the same mistake that I made," he said. "Keep Him at the center of your life. I hope that you put God number one in your life, so that when you have that crisis and that trial, you don't feel the guilt that I felt. Hopefully I can make a difference in your life."

After the video, Rogers came back up and confirmed that Keith's perspective in that video was unchanged until the day he died. He never stopped seeking the Lord first, his pastor said, and he never succumbed to bitterness, anger, or self-pity. He held fast to the belief that God was using every painful aspect of his disease for His glory.

"Keith's constant prayer was that each of you would discover what he had discovered, that the goal and the prize that satisfies in life is not ultimately found in a place called Omaha, but it is found in a faith that sustains you through thick and thin, in tragedy and in difficult times, and that is found in the person of Jesus Christ," Rogers said.

When the two-hour funeral had concluded and the guests had trickled out of the Oakmont sanctuary, Keith's family had less than an hour to regroup before starting the next service, at the ECU baseball stadium. And as they drove the two miles from the church to Clark-LeClair Stadium, many of the mourners were thinking about the last time they had sat in that venue to honor Keith, just over a year earlier. It was March 4, 2005—the first game in the new stadium that was named for Keith and embodied his dream for ECU baseball.

That morning before the Pirates faced Michigan in the brand-new facility in an annual tournament called the Keith LeClair Classic, J.D. and Audrey threw out symbolic first pitches and Keith was honored at home plate with a commemorative plaque and gold roses. Those first innings in the venue were played seven years after Keith had sat in a Baton Rouge restaurant on the heels of a dramatic ECU victory over LSU and discussed a new stadium with some Pirate backers. He also kick-started the capital campaign for the space in 2001, the same year he was diagnosed with ALS.

In a statement read by Chuck Young during the ceremony, Keith expressed his gratitude toward those who had propelled his dream forward and stated the significance the stadium would always have for his family. "How much longer I can continue living on a ventilator, only God truly knows," he said. "But when that final day does come, my two kids Audrey and J.D. can always look up at Clark-LeClair Stadium and know two things. One, when they see the Clark name, they will see the ultimate sacrifice of giving and sharing to a family during difficult times. Second, when they see the name LeClair, they will know to never ever give up and to always follow your dreams and visions."

The lead gift of $1.5 million was given by ECU supporter Bill Clark, who shares the stadium's name with LeClair. Clark always wanted his donation to be a means to honor the man who sparked the stadium project. "One of the reasons why

I wanted to support this project was to get Keith's name on the stadium as it should be," Clark said when the $10 million project was completed. "I'm not sure one person has done as much for one individual sport as Keith has for our baseball program. I wanted there to be a legacy for Keith at ECU."

It was into that brick-and-mortar legacy that hundreds of fans and friends filed that hot July day for the "Celebration of Life." Joey Perry, the ECU groundskeeper and one of Keith's closest friends, had been busy putting some special touches on the field. Large white "23s" were painted behind home plate and beside both baselines, and LeClair's number was also stamped in the infield dirt. Those "23s" were reflected everywhere in the stands, on the jerseys countless fans wore, and on the signs they held up.

The informal stadium service opened with remarks from Jeff Charles, the broadcasting voice of the ECU Pirates and the host of the ceremony. Charles called first for Keith's coaching colleagues to approach the mike and share their memories and insights, and the coaches would be followed by former players, around thirty of whom had gathered in the dugout.

The first speaker that evening was Tommy Eason, Keith's former assistant who was still part of the ECU staff at that time. Eason was emotional as he remembered Keith as a mentor who gave him a chance at coaching when he had no experience. "Because of Keith, I was able to coach these players, which has been an honor," he said. "That's what it's been all about. That's what college baseball, in my opinion, is all about, being able to provide guidance, leadership, and hopefully, opportunity. That's really what Keith meant to me."

Todd Raleigh, who followed LeClair as the head coach at Western, remembered how often Leggett would hold Keith up as an example when Raleigh was a freshman Catamount and Keith was a senior. "Every time I did something wrong, Coach Leggett would pull me aside and say, 'You need to be

Family friend Chuck Young reads a statement from Lynn LeClair at the stadium service as Lynn watches on.

more like Keith,'" Raleigh said. "The true character of a man is at his lowest point. When Keith contracted ALS, he never changed."

ECU coach Billy Godwin, who had taken over for Randy Mazey in 2005, also spoke about his own responsibility to help fulfill and complete the dreams that Keith planted in the Pirate baseball program. "I share the same vision for East Carolina baseball as Keith LeClair shared, that one day the Pirates will play in Rosenblatt Stadium in Omaha," Godwin said. "I know when I make that trip to Omaha, that Number 23 is going to be sitting right there on the bench beside me."

The next group of men to speak formed a meaningful bridge between the coaches and the former players. They were the five ex-LeClair players who had gone on to their own collegiate coaching careers. George Whitfield put that accomplishment in perspective years later, when he speculated that in his own decades as a head coach, just one or two young men becoming Division I coaches would be considered a success. In just four years at the helm at ECU, LeClair had produced five.

Not only were all of those alumni making their mark as young baseball coaches, they were all staying connected with each other as friends and former teammates. And as they grieved the man who had inspired their career paths, they shared a dream that would serve as the ultimate tribute to the man they so admired. Joe Hastings, who had started at Virginia Military Institute and had just accepted an assistant coaching job at Boston College the month of the funeral, sketched out that dream for the crowd that day at the stadium: "Coach LeClair had a dream of being in Omaha," Hastings said. "There are five of us who played here who are carrying on that dream. One of these days, you're going to see five LeClair guys in Omaha together. That's going to be a fantastic day."

After the young coaches spoke, a seemingly endless stream of former players came, one at a time, to the microphone. Their remembrances were heartfelt and often humorous, as they remembered the hard-nosed New Englander who had led them on early morning workouts that closely resembled Army boot camp. Amid the stories, many were able to verbalize why they were different men because their paths had crossed Keith LeClair's.

Former ECU catcher Jason Howard recalled a time when Keith scolded him for casually flipping the ball up in the air after he made a third out, as if he were rubbing the opposing team's face in his success. Coach told him never to do anything that would show disrespect for the other team. "What he was best at was teaching us lessons," he said. "His legacy will be defined by what he taught us off the field and the men he made of us." Jeremy Schumacher, a pitcher from 1997 to 2000, said: "Most people don't get to know their hero. Their hero might be whoever, an actor, the president. I got to live and breathe and sweat with the hero of my lifetime. I count myself extremely lucky."

When every former Pirate had spoken his tribute and the

fans had filed quietly out of the sparking new venue, Greenville's official day of mourning Keith LeClair was over. But for weeks on the East Carolina athletics website, everyone from close friends to outright strangers took the time to write messages to the LeClair family on the official tribute page that was set up for Keith. More than 400 people wrote their feelings on the website, including nine different Division I head baseball coaches.

Out of hundreds, a couple of messages from men who loved Keith like a brother for decades stood out, because they were written directly to him. From former WCU teammate and coaching colleague Todd Raleigh: "Where you are now is like being in Omaha every day." And from childhood buddy Dean Gay: "I'll keep my arm loose for some BP later."

After throwing the doors open to the city of Greenville and the ECU community on July 21, the circle closed to include only the family and close friends for Keith's burial—on Sunday, July 23. Young was openly frustrated a few times when Keith's date to turn off the ventilator had to be moved to accommodate schedules or conflicts, but he admits he marveled when he realized that his friend would be buried on the 23rd of the month—yet another "23 story" for a growing collection.

Even though the notices stated that a private burial was planned, more than 100 friends and family members made the trip to upstate South Carolina to be there when Keith was laid to rest. Sherry Odom was there, and she went to the Winchesters' family church, Shady Grove Baptist, for the service that morning and came back to tell Lynn that the pastor had preached on Psalm 23. The church members put together a lunch for the family and out-of-town friends after the service, and then the group went to Hillcrest Memorial Park in Pickens for a short service led by Chuck Young. Matt Stillwell, the country music singer who once played baseball for Keith at Western, sang a song at the graveside.

The services and burial offered some degree of closure and healing to the LeClairs, but there was still one crucial place waiting to say its own goodbyes. A special memorial service was planned for August 13 in Walpole. Someone had given Lynn and the kids tickets to see Keith's favorite major-league baseball team—the Red Sox—and they stopped to see the game on their trip North.

The speakers at the Walpole service, which was held at the historic Congregational Church downtown, were Keith's old high school baseball coach Hank Beecher and high school friend Joe Milliken. Jeff Campbell, Keith's childhood best friend and neighbor, initially agreed to say something but found when the day came that the pain was too raw. Campbell's mother, Pat, stepped up instead, and spoke for the family, recalling the boy who was like another son to her and the memories of him that will always seem like a part of their home.

Beecher coached many hundreds of young men, and no coach ever wants to stand up to speak at a player's funeral. He was nervous as he considered what to say about one of his favorite athletes from back in the 1980s, that boy who wanted to know every nuance of baseball. "I talked about his faith in God, and how he achieved things in his life that maybe most people thought he wouldn't," Beecher said. "The bravery he fought his disease with was no surprise to me. He tackled that the same way he tackled other obstacles in his life. He just went full bore until he couldn't go any more."

For Milliken, the most memorable part of that day wasn't standing up in front of people and talking about Keith, even though he did get a chance to share his memories. The thing he will never forget was seeing Keith projected on a screen, sharing the same Oakmont Baptist testimony that was shown at the funeral in Greenville. While the people at Keith's North Carolina church had heard him speak about his faith before, his childhood friends were thunderstruck at the poise and boldness they saw in that video.

"I'm watching that screen, and I'm listening to him, and my mouth was hanging open," Milliken said. "And I remembered what Dean Gay had told me, about how much he had grown as a person. The Keith I know, he wasn't that outspoken. And the way he was talking and what he was saying, I just remember sitting at that service and going, 'My Lord, look what he's done.' I can't believe how much he transformed himself to be what he had to be, a good coach and a good recruiter.'"

In Walpole, in Cullowhee, in Greenville, gaping holes stood in the place of a life extraordinarily lived. With four different funerals behind her, Lynn needed to turn to J.D. and Audrey, to help them work through their grief and discover their new "normal." Under the watchful eye of her concerned friends, she returned home to shop for school supplies and get the kids mentally prepared for the third and sixth grades.

Jack Leggett comforts Lynn LeClair at the "Celebration of Life" memorial service held on July 20 at Clark-LeClair Stadium.

10
Legacy

GREENVILLE WAS KEITH'S HOME FOR THE LAST NINE YEARS of his life, and it was a place that offered him professional triumph when he was healthy and abiding love and support when he was ill. After a summer defined by an extended goodbye, the LeClair family was faced with the next test—figuring out how to press on in Greenville without Keith. The school year brought some semblance of routine, but those fall months are a blur to most of the LeClairs' inner circle.

Suddenly the house was quieter than it had been in years, and Lynn had time on her hands that had been consumed by caring for her husband. Not long after Keith died, one of the family cats was killed by the electric garage door, and that tragedy evoked the emotions of the mid-summer. Through his tears that night, J.D. looked around him and asked his mom, bewildered, "Why isn't anyone coming?"

Audrey was starting middle school, and she found diversions in friends and activities there. J.D. was occupied too, but he was the family member who most often expressed a desire to leave Greenville and move to upstate South Carolina. "He had it in his mind that we should just pack up and go," Lynn said. His wish had little to do with Greenville and everything to do with his grandfather, now the most influential man in his life. "My grandpa, him and my dad meant just everything to me when I was little," J.D. explained.

During the years of his dad's illness, J.D. had plenty of surrogates to fill in where Keith could not—playing ball in

Audrey and J.D. LeClair walk out to the mound to throw out the first pitches to open the LeClair Classic baseball tournament, February 2006.

the backyard, taking him to baseball practice, wrestling on the rug. But now that his dad was gone, he seemed keenly aware that only Grandpa Doug could really fill that void. Lynn knew, too, that the most supportive place for them was near extended family, but she was torn about leaving the place whose people had loved them deeply and met so many of their needs. It was a sentiment she expressed memorably at the Clark-LeClair Stadium memorial service, in her statement read by Chuck Young.

"The topography of Eastern North Carolina doesn't allow for mountains," she said. "But after living and becoming a part of this area, I've realized that the people of Eastern North Carolina are its mountains."

There was nothing easy about leaving the city that had been home for a decade, but in the winter of 2008, a year and a half after Keith's death, the LeClairs packed up and moved to tiny Shady Grove, South Carolina. The house they would settle in had belonged to Lynn's grandparents, and it was directly across the street from her parents, leaving an open door for J.D. to zip across the street multiple times a day to hang out with his grandpa. The new arrangement also allowed space for Audrey, an avid equestrian, to keep her horse in a stable behind the house and ride every day.

Just minutes from that house sits Lake Calton, a wooded 900-acre property owned by Lynn's family. It was, without a doubt, Keith's favorite place in the world. He never knew what his coaching career would hold, Lynn said, but he was absolutely sure that when he had coached his last game he wanted to retire to Lake Calton, where bountiful hunting and fishing were just outside the door of the cabin that stood on the land. J.D. loved to go out there too, and he was always aware of every living creature in the vicinity. A true outdoorsman in the mold of his dad, he was a boy who, when he went to Walt Disney World for the first time, was mostly interested in the Animal Kingdom. When visitors came into his South Carolina home looking to know more about his father, the first items J.D. wanted to show them were the stuffed deer heads and other hunting mementos upstairs. Lynn came to realize that this was another reason J.D. was determined to move—as much as he loved sports himself, he identified with his dad more strongly on the banks of Lake Calton than on a baseball field.

Just a few months after Lynn and the kids moved to South Carolina, her father was admitted to the hospital for chest pains, and he ended up having bypass surgery. After he recovered, Lynn redoubled her prayers for his continued health and strength because she knew how much all of them—but most of all J.D.—needed him. Not long after Doug's surgery, one of Lynn's cousins who lived nearby was killed in a car accident. Those trials, coupled with the major renovations to their house she was overseeing, were sources of stress as she continued to mourn Keith.

Back in Greenville, Keith's former caregivers were also trying to pick up the pieces and to fill the gaping holes left in their lives and their schedules. Every Monday night, Jerry

Greene had to talk himself out of getting in the car and driving to Keith's house. For Sherry Odom, healing seemed like too tall an order in the months after Keith's death; she settled for putting one foot in front of the other. "I just had to keep going," she said. "I don't think I have completely grieved a normal grief through it all, because Keith would never let us grieve. And after, I felt like I couldn't grieve because of Lynn and the children. And for a long time I was completely unemotional about anything, because if one thing happened I feel like everything would have come out."

Still, as the sun continued to come up each morning and Sherry and Mike started to dream about opening their own physical therapy practice, it was Keith's example that emboldened them to step out. Mike's job had been eliminated, and they started looking for a place to start their own business. At one point they had started preparing for the clinic, but they had second thoughts about the risk and put all of their equipment in storage. A few months later, they rented a space, unpacked the equipment and launched Greenville Physical Therapy with just eight weeks of preparation.

Framed clippings and photos of Keith hang on the wall of the Greenville Physical Therapy treatment room, a memorial to the man whose courage helped set the trajectory of the Odoms' professional leap of faith. They never talked specifically to Keith about the clinic, but they knew without question what he would have said about the opportunity. "If Keith could do what he did, anything was possible," Sherry Odom said. "He gave me courage. Keith, to me, was the strongest human being I've ever known."

All over the country, friends felt Keith's absence and honored his memory in various ways. Some went to the East Carolina athletics website regularly to watch a video tribute that was posted there. Others recalled Keith's battle when they felt the temptation to fixate about their own circumstances. "It reinforces that there are people out there who can take on the world," said former WCU player Roy Hurst, who sees his own adverse circumstances through a different lens after watching LeClair battle ALS. "He didn't complain. Right now I'm in Florida, and it's drizzling, and that's putting me in a foul mood."

Each time Keith's college teammate Paul Menhart heard of an ALS diagnosis through the grapevine or on the news, his thoughts went to his old college coach: "It kind of sets you back a little bit, and your day changes," he said.

Countless recipients of Keith's e-mails credited him with a newfound Christian faith, or a renewed understanding of the God who had guided them for years. East Carolina wasn't the most productive professional stop in Kevin Mc-Mullan's coaching journey, but he is sure that he was brought to Greenville for a different reason. "More than anything else, I learned more about my faith during those years," said Mc-Mullan, who has carried the words of Psalm 23 in his memory ever since Keith pointed the passage out to him in an e-mail.

Others who knew Keith turned the constant reminders of his life into a concrete legacy. Matt Stillwell was known at Western Carolina as a Catamount baseball player with a guitar, but he went on to make a name for himself in country music. With hit songs like "Shine" drawing attention, Stillwell has opened up for the likes of Alan Jackson, but his former college coach and the disease that claimed his life have never been far from his mind. He has played dozens of benefit concerts for ALS research over the years, and in 2008 he founded Shinefest, a country music festival in Western North Carolina whose proceeds benefit, in part, the ALS Foundation.

But of all the people who remember and honor Keith in their daily routines, none have more opportunities than the men whose careers revolve around baseball. Four years after his death, at least a dozen of Keith's former players or teammates from WCU or ECU were coaching on the collegiate level, with others coaching the minor leagues or at the youth level. One former Pirate, Chad Tracy, had a productive major-league career with the Arizona Diamondbacks.

When he was busy with his Eyegaze computer, tuning into six or seven baseball games at a time, Keith was looking for scores and stats from specific teams—the ones coached by "his boys." Once when Stuart Robertson was helping Audrey write a school paper about her father, the teacher asked Audrey to include more statistics and details about Keith's career. When Stuart pressed Keith for that information, though, he said he didn't keep up with his own stats. But he made up for it by meticulously following the careers of men who had discovered, as he did years earlier, the joys of leading and inspiring young baseball players. He advised them as they applied for openings, and he was quick to write countless reference letters for former Pirates on his computer. "He always wanted to know what he could do to help," said James Molinari.

The most striking cross-section of Keith's coaching family tree is the five members of the 2000 team, all close friends in college and beyond, who found Division I coaching opportunities around the same time: Bryant Ward, Cliff Godwin, Erik Bakich, Nick Schnabel, and Joseph Hastings. In the first seven years of their coaching careers, they combined to coach at fifteen different Division I colleges, including baseball powerhouses like Louisiana State University, Cal State Fullerton, and Clemson. In 2009, Bakich was the first of the group to earn a head coaching position, becoming the skipper at the University of Maryland at the age of thirty-one.

Each coach has developed his own distinct leadership style, but each can also identify the LeClair tributaries that flow in and around his daily dealings with players and recruits. They see Keith in their work ethic that was sharpened in those dawn boot camp workouts, in their tendency to take a chance on a kid who is short on accolades but long on grit. Their hope is that his spirit lives on as they strive for

*A group of former Pirate teammates-turned-coaches
pose at Nick Schnabel's wedding, December 2007. L–R:
Cliff Godwin, Erik Bakich, Schnabel, James Molinari,
and Bryant Ward.*

excellence in coaching and courage in their daily lives.

"He's the reason why I'm sitting here today," said Hastings, who still has to stop himself regularly from calling his old coach to share a triumph or ask a question. "I'm a finger of Coach LeClair and a branch of the tree. All of the other guys that are coaching are doing the same things that he did."

They may not get to share their stories with Keith, but the five coaches have always talked to each other regularly. They have stood as groomsmen in each other's weddings, rejoiced in the births of babies, and occasionally even coached across the field from each other. They laugh together when they hear themselves parrot "LeClairisms" like, "We've got to get our feet back underneath us." When they were players, they puzzled over that statement, but Schnabel found himself exhorting players with that very phrase while he was coaching at Liberty University. In the summer of 2009, they all celebrated Bakich's hiring at Maryland and Schnabel's decision to leave Liberty for the assistant coaching position back where it all started—at East Carolina.

Schnabel loved Liberty, and he had an exceptional relationship with head coach Jim Toman, whose spiritual life was deepened years earlier by the e-mails he received from Keith LeClair. There were precious few job offers that would have pulled him away from Lynchburg, but one of those was certainly the chance to trace his journey full circle back to Pirate Country. "When this (ECU job) came open, it was a no-brainer for me," said Schnabel, who knew he was in the right place when he heard the ECU head coach refer to favorable recruits as "blue collar" like Keith used to.

Before he was introduced as Maryland's head coach, Bakich wrote a statement describing his debt to LeClair and his belief that his career would have taken a different trajectory altogether if he had not spent two seasons at ECU. "I played for Coach Keith LeClair at East Carolina, which has been the greatest baseball honor of my life," Bakich wrote. "Those two years with Coach LeClair were the defining moments of my development not only as an athlete, but most importantly as a person and as a man. He taught his players the true meaning of mental toughness and inspired his teams to out-train, out-hustle, and out-work the competition, as well as a fearless, hard-nosed, aggressive, blue-color attitude that refused to stop fighting no matter how many times we got knocked down. He then lived those principles and values he instilled in his players and showed what true character is as he fought a five-year battle with ALS. He passed away in July 2006, but Keith LeClair will always be my hero and inspiration, the reason I became a coach, and the reason six of my teammates at ECU are now coaching in Division I baseball, continuing the legacy of one of the greatest men that has ever lived."

Whenever possible, the coaches in the Keith network wear number 23 in his memory, and like others who knew Keith, they have seen that number pop up in the strangest of places. One of the most dramatic stories came when Godwin was coaching at LSU. It was June 2008, and LSU seemed to be unbeatable. Riding the nation's longest winning streak, the Tigers made it to the NCAA Super Regional against the University of California-Irvine. UC-Irvine won the first game, breaking LSU's streak, and one more loss would mean the end of the Tigers' season. Wearing 23, Godwin was coaching third base like his mentor had, and he remembers saying, "Hey, Coach, help us out with this one." They came from behind and won, then dominated the next game for a trip to the College World Series.

It was only after that postseason odyssey that Godwin understood the greatest milestone of LSU's season. He wasn't keeping count in the middle of the winning streak, but later he realized that his team had lost just one game in months against UC-Irvine to stop the streak at 23 games. To Godwin, it was a reminder that Keith continued to inspire and lead.

In addition to those who went into college coaching, one player from that 2000 squad went on to coach a minor-league team, one founded a youth baseball league, and another went from ECU to a successful major-league baseball career. Clayton McCullough turned a short minor-league playing career into a series of coaching gigs with teams in the Toronto Blue Jays farm system. James Molinari tried college coaching, too, but he found his niche in leading younger players, founding a youth league that fields six travel teams for ten- to fifteen-year-olds. Tracy, who graduated the year after Molinari, was selected in the seventh round of the 2001 Major League Baseball draft and was called up by the Arizona Diamondbacks in 2004. In his second year in the bigs, Tracy had the seventh best batting average in the major leagues, a .308. He spent six seasons in Arizona and filed for free agency at the end of the 2009 season.

Other ex-Pirates have joined the coaching fraternity in the years since those friends tested the waters. Ben Sanderson, a 2003 ECU graduate, spent three years as a Pirate assistant before taking a job at Florida Atlantic University. Like his teammates, Sanderson coaches in the welcome shadow of the man who once convinced him that his role as a pinch runner was essential to the success of his team. "I use stuff that I learned from Coach every day," Sanderson said. "The four years that I played under him made me the person I am and influenced my character. Just to see the level it takes to be excellent in college baseball, the work it requires, it affected me."

The disproportionate number of Coach's protégés in the coaching ranks has given rise to further examination of LeClair's leadership model. It's a trend that can't be explained only by his win-loss record or by his valiant public fight against ALS. As they pursue excellence on the teams they lead, these young coaches are starting to see that they are driven by the desire to fashion an intense, single-minded family that exemplifies every sports cliché about team trumping individual. They know such an ideal exists, because each of them was once a part of it.

"I don't think it's necessarily baseball-related," Molinari said. "I don't think it's because we played for Coach and now we have an increased love for baseball. I don't think that has anything to do with it. I think it has everything to do with, 'How on earth am I best friends with guys that I couldn't stand when I first came out here [to ECU]?' That camaraderie makes you want to stay in baseball, to try to achieve that again."

The strands of the LeClair coaching web all reach back to purple and gold uniforms, but they aren't all from ECU. A dizzying number of Keith's former players and teammates from Western Carolina also pursued coaching careers, from small colleges to Division I powerhouses. For a while at Georgia Southern University, both head coach Rodney Hennon (who succeeded Keith as the WCU head coach in 1997) and assistants Jason Beverlin and Mike Tidick were former

Catamounts. Beverlin later went on to join LeClair's former teammate Todd Raleigh at the University of Tennessee,
where Raleigh was hired as the head coach in 2007. "It's a big
web," said Raleigh, who spent one year as Keith's assistant at
ECU and then succeeded Hennon as the Western head coach
in 2000.

At least two college coaches who didn't even play under
Keith believed that he is the only reason they're not putting
on a suit and tie every morning. Raleigh might have reached
the pinnacle as the Tennessee head coach, but in 1993 he was
an aimless ex-ball player hanging out at his parents' house in
Vermont. He had spent a couple of years playing in the Red
Sox farm system off and on and had suffered a shoulder injury that led to surgery. His playing career seemed to be over,
but he had no idea what he would do next. Keith, a role model to the younger player during their Western Carolina days,
tracked him down during that time and took him on a New
England fishing trip. What Keith proposed as they fished,
Raleigh remembered, caught him completely off guard.

"I want you to come here (to WCU) to coach," LeClair said.

"That's not really what I want to do," said Raleigh, who
had never once considered coaching before that day. "I don't
have a place to live."

"I've got that covered."

"I don't know how I'll pay tuition."

"I've got that covered."

LeClair had arranged for Raleigh to have a graduate as-
sistantship, earning his master's degree while he coached. He
had every angle covered, but Raleigh was still hesitant. Keith
called him four times in the next two days, until Raleigh finally relented and moved back South. It was the first of four
assistant coaching jobs, which led to the top post at WCU
and then to Tennessee. Like LeClair, Raleigh was profoundly
impacted by Jack Leggett when both played under him, but
his adult professional life began with LeClair, who seemed to

fashion Raleigh's career out of his will alone.

From his office across town from Clark-LeClair Stadium, Tommy Eason recalled the time when he considered selling insurance. Instead he became a coach, thanks to the young newcomer who put part of his new team in the hands of an ex-catcher he didn't even know. LeClair hired Eason in 1997 as an assistant at the recommendation of long-time ECU administrator Henry Van Sant, and like Raleigh, Eason was tempted by the prospect of tuition help for his master's program. Eason spent eight years as an ECU assistant coach before taking the head job at Pitt Community College in Greenville.

After Eason had been a graduate assistant under LeClair for just a year, LeClair promoted him to the vital pitching coach position, trusting in Eason's potential more than his actual accomplishments to that point. In those early years, Eason was continually struck by LeClair's willingness to let Eason have the reins and learn from the inevitable mistakes any rookie makes. "He let me do my job," Eason said. "Here his name is on the line, more than mine is. And to give me that leeway was pretty special. And it's obviously transcended into something that's been good."

Keith Shumate, who came into the Western Carolina baseball program with LeClair and was put through pool conditioning with him to get both players stronger, is coaching just three hours east of Greenville, at North Carolina A&T University. It's a small historically black college, and when the opportunity arose Shumate remembers LeClair trying to dissuade him from taking a team that had gone 4–45 the previous season. Shumate took the job anyway, and added digits to that win column every year. It's still an uphill coaching climb, but Shumate is committed to heeding his old college buddy's warning to make his Christian faith the foundation for every aspect of his life as a coach, husband, and father. Even toiling away at an underfunded program that rarely compiles a winning record, he knows now that coaches can have an eternal impact.

"Keith's experiences and his devotionals, they gave me real-life confirmation that God can use you and use you mightily," Shumate said. "One time I told him, 'God laid it on my heart to say this. You were a great baseball coach, and you were a great baseball player, but if you were only a great coach and player, hundreds of people might know you. But now, because of this, millions might know you.'"

It's an intricate web of baseball coaches that would be nearly impossible to trace with accuracy, especially because coaches are always on the move to better opportunities. But all over the nation, coaches are pushing players to heights they never dreamed they could scale, chasing excellence, and trying to make tough decisions with integrity. The legacy humming under those player meetings, that batting practice and those late-night bus rides is the indelible mark of Keith LeClair.

From Jack Leggett at his perennial Clemson powerhouse on down to a young assistant with only a few years of experience, every coach who ever spent time in LeClair's sphere of influence carries Keith's most fervent baseball dream—a trip to the College World Series. Some have made it, some are in programs that seem a far cry from national dominance, but for all, the hope of Omaha is—as it was for Keith—undimmed. And as those five buddies expressed at Keith's stadium memorial service, the ultimate hope is that they will one day be at Omaha's Rosenblatt Stadium together—competitors bound by something incalculably bigger than baseball.

Afterword

JUNE 1, 2009, WAS A NIGHT MADE POSSIBLE BY KEITH LECLAIR'S big dream about a fantastic baseball stadium. It was one of the most unforgettable nights in East Carolina baseball history, a transcendent victory that certainly belonged to Coach Billy Godwin and his players, but still evoked strong memories of Number 23.

The ECU Pirates had put together a 42–17 record in the regular season, and they were ranked in the top twenty in every major poll. The table seemed to be set for the culmination of a goal birthed in 1999, when Keith and some ECU boosters first batted around the idea of a new stadium. If the project was undertaken with excellence and the Pirates continued to win, they knew that Clark-LeClair Stadium could soon be the perfect place to host an NCAA Regional.

Five years after the first game was played on that diamond, the NCAA Baseball Selection Committee announced the regional pairings on live television, with every Pirate player gathered around to watch. The announcement was the very one the Pirate Nation had been hoping to hear: East Carolina would be the host and the number one seed, with Binghamton, George Mason, and South Carolina coming to play.

Before the first pitch was even thrown in the regional, Tim Sinicki came to town and set into motion a series of Keith LeClair reminiscences. Sinicki was one of Keith's buddies in college, when both were just trying to make their mark on the small college stage at Western Carolina. A New York native, Sinicki gave Keith rides home to New Hampshire a couple of times. Suddenly, those twenty years were a vapor. Sinicki's Binghamton University Bearcats were in their first-

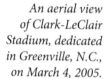

*An aerial view
of Clark-LeClair
Stadium, dedicated
in Greenville, N.C.,
on March 4, 2005.*

ever regional, and they were being sent to play it in the stadium named after the friend he once regarded like a brother. At the banquet ECU held for all visiting players and coaches, Sinicki made dozens of connections with people who, if not for their mutual love for Keith, would have been strangers.

"I could talk forever about Keith," Sinicki said from his Greenville hotel that week before the regional. "I'm happy to let people here know that he touched so many lives outside of Greenville, that people all over have a connection with him. So many people have come up and talked to me. You share the same thoughts and feelings about Keith that they had, and you really start to put the pieces together."

ECU might have been the number one seed, but South Carolina players had been treating them like an easy win in the media, like a small bump the Gamecocks needed to roll over on their road to Omaha. As the tournament got underway on May 29, ECU and USC eliminated the other two teams and were left to face each other. The Gamecocks dominated the first game, putting themselves just one win away from advancing. But then the Pirates came back in the next game to edge them out 8–6 and set up a winner-takes-all final on June 1.

Before 5,047 fans, the Pirates struggled early, trailing 6–0 into the fifth inning. ECU rallied, but they were still behind 9–6 at the top of the ninth inning. Two Pirates drew walks in that inning, setting up Devin Harris as the hero. Harris hit a home run to tie the game at 9 and send the game into extra innings. With the crowd on its feet and the fans worked into a frenzy, Harris turned in the sequel of his hero drama with a deep single in the tenth that was just enough to score Kyle Roller. The Pirates were champions of their regional, and they would head to Chapel Hill the next weekend to take on the University of North Carolina in the Super Regional.

Those 2009 Pirates couldn't pull out another miracle against North Carolina, but the magical strands of that June night became a permanent part of the tapestry that knits Keith in with other Pirate coaches, past and present. His legacy in that group will certainly be the players who have gone on to coach young men at colleges across the country, and the beautiful stadium that bears his name. But the story of Keith LeClair and his influence on ECU baseball goes deeper than the sport and veers into territory like character, courage, devotion, and sacrifice. And few people in Greenville have a better handle on that legacy than Billy Godwin.

Godwin took the head coaching job at ECU in 2005, and that summer he went to visit his predecessor. The two had a professional relationship prior to Godwin's hiring, because Godwin was the head coach at nearby Louisburg College, and LeClair knew Louisburg was fertile ground for strong junior college prospects. He was taking over at ECU for Randy Mazey, who had been the head coach for three seasons. Keith was still there in town, still a palpable presence, but Godwin had every right to come in and create his own system with little thought to Keith and his story.

Mazey had instituted an annual award, given to a deserving senior, giving that player the right to wear 23 for his final year as a Pirate. Godwin had a choice about whether to continue that young tradition, and there were some advising him to end it. He did exactly the opposite. Early in his tenure, he had a meeting with the first three recipients of the award—Ben Sanderson, Jamie Paige, and Brian Cavanaugh—and asked

In February 2009 Brandon Henderson (left), the seventh
ECU player to be awarded the Number 23 jersey,
receives his jersey from Drew Schieber (right), who wore
the number in 2008.

them to craft a list of criteria that any young man who wears 23 should have. Godwin took that input and amplified the program's emphasis on the honor so that today it is the highest designation a Pirate baseball player can be given. "What I wanted to do was elevate it, so that twenty years from now it's as important as it was twenty years ago," said Godwin, who had followed legendary coach Russ Frazier at Louisburg College and took care to honor him in his years there. "Anybody that followed the program realized what an impact Keith had in such a short time. I believe that you should embrace legacies, anywhere you go."

Sanderson, who played for Keith for three seasons, was chosen in 2003 as the first player to wear Number 23. It was an unparalleled honor, and when Godwin approached him, Paige, and Cavanaugh two years later, looking for advice about whether to continue the jersey dedications or retire LeClair's number, they were certain that the best way to honor Coach's memory was to keep that number moving, from one class of Pirates to the next. "I wanted it to be such an honor that when freshmen come into the program, they want to be the type of person that is capable of living up to wearing that jersey," Sanderson said.

The three former Pirates collaborated on the words they wanted engraved on the special plaque that is awarded to each recipient of the 23 jersey. The award reads, "For every East Carolina Baseball team there is a certain player who embodies the spirit and determination of Keith LeClair. A player who works hard, has internal drive and strives daily to play like a champion." At the heart of the selection process is the search for a player who can squeeze every last drop out of his store of ability. If a player wears that purple and gold "23," it should go without saying that he personifies what Keith used to call "blue collar," or "a grinder."

Anyone who ever watched Keith LeClair play or coach baseball saw him maximize his talent that way. Omaha was an audacious goal, but Keith had no interest in small wishes or artificially imposed limits. If there was a limit to what an individual or a team could achieve, they were going to find it themselves, by slamming up against the boundary wall.

So when his battle left the baseball field and moved to an eternal arena, the same principles held. His body was broken, his speech was gone, and he was unable to breathe on his own, but he refused to accept either pity or low expectations. ALS was a tragedy for Keith and his family and friends, but he somehow managed to accept that reality and make it transformational for himself and for everyone around him. As he pressed on in his faith and looked for ways to share his unfathomable hope, Keith became a different kind of coach.

"I don't think Coach LeClair could help but have an impact on people—as a coach, father and husband, friend, and teacher when he was sick," Sanderson said. "It was just inherent in his nature to have an impact on people. He was a coach right up until the end."

Acknowledgments

LIKE KEITH DID BEFORE ME, I HAVE TO START BY GIVING glory to God. The path of this book was marked by the Lord opening one door after another, and it was clearly He who gave me the strength and direction to undertake this project. I even had a few "23" stories of my own to spur me along. I am also indebted to all of the generous people who gave their time and recollections because they believed Keith's story should be told.

Along the way, I heard many accounts of Lynn's selflessness and courage in the midst of dark valleys. But I didn't need to be told about that courage, because I experienced it so many times firsthand. Through face-to-face visits, manuscript mailings, and countless phone calls, she sacrificed her privacy and her precious memories and trusted me to handle them with care. By sharing from her heart and going to places that are still raw, she demonstrated selflessness and love for Keith and set an example for Audrey and J.D., who also let me into their lives when they could have easily decided to keep their memories of their dad private.

Other family members in both South Carolina and New Hampshire showed me great kindness. I am indebted to Doug, Donna, Kevin, and Andy, but especially to Doris, who never wearied of my questions and requests. Through the strength of a mother's love, she read manuscripts, collected photos, found phone numbers, and helped me keep the lines of communication to Walpole wide open.

All told, I interviewed sixty-three people for this book, and all were eager to share their stories of Keith, even when they had to talk through their tears. More than one tough baseball player or coach wept when they remembered Keith, but they were unfailingly generous with those tender memories. I am especially grateful to Kevin Haverty, Keith's high school basketball coach in New Hampshire, who welcomed me into his home even though he was waging his own intense battle with cancer. Sadly, Coach Haverty died in July 2009 before the book was completed, but his generosity of spirit is memorialized through his words in these pages.

Some of those dozens stand out because I called them again and again, and several read copies of the drafts to catch my baseball, history, or editing errors. Chuck Young, George Whitfield, and Jody Jones, as well as doctor friends who checked my medical descriptions, are some of the people I am indebted to for their aid in the editing process.

Many people helped with the collection and scanning of pictures for the book, notably Malcolm Gray at East Carolina, Joe Milliken in Walpole, and Jason Mills at ASAP Photo in Greenville. And Lisa Stroud proved time and again what it really means to pour out your gifts to help a friend, as she tirelessly edited manuscripts and then proved what a multi-talented woman she is by designing a wonderful cover.

I am part of an incredible community, and I wish I could remember or find space for every friend who supported, prayed, kept my children, or offered me a place to work. Special thanks to the Duke and Johnson families for providing quiet space for me to write when the chaos level in my own home became prohibitive.

To Kit Sublett, my publisher, I am amazed when I consider the Lord's plan for a twenty-five-year friendship that started in a Northwest Houston Young Life club. Only a creative God could take us on such an adventure.

Finally, to my husband Sid, and our children Preston, Holly, Benjamin, and Jake—you were my best cheerleaders, even when I couldn't give you a goodnight hug because I had stolen away for some writing time. The entire Bradsher family made sacrifices so that this big dream could become a reality, and you energized me with your love every step of the way. I love you with all my heart.

Bethany Bradsher
Greenville, North Carolina

Keith's Devotionals

IN 2003, AFTER CLOSE TO A YEAR OF SILENCE, KEITH
LeClair opened the doors of communication through the
Eyegaze computer. He used the technology for all kinds of
things—to check baseball scores, write e-mails, order gifts for
his family—but the most lasting purpose of the Eyegaze had
to be the Christian devotionals Keith penned and e-mailed
to family and friends all over the country.

Touched by his insights in the midst of a dark valley, the
recipients of the devotionals forwarded them to countless
others, and the devotionals soon became a lifeline of
encouragement for untold people. What follows is a selection
of ten of those writings that represent Keith's unyielding faith
and his eternal perspective during the years of his illness.

November 2002
Are We a Little Like Goliath?

We all know the story of David and Goliath. How David, just a small young man in stature, slew Goliath with a sling and a smooth rock. Here Goliath was a giant whom everyone deemed invincible, not only in the eyes of the Philistines, but even amongst the Jews. Nobody thought Goliath could be conquered, not even Goliath himself. You could say Goliath was cocky and had good reason. But Goliath, as well as David, provides a powerful message to us all. You're probably asking yourself, "How can Goliath, whom David killed with one stone, provide any kind of message to me of any significance?" I felt that very same way until I really thought about the whole story and put both sides in context.

There truly are two messages in this one story. The first is David, the underdog, and the second is Goliath, whom everyone thought was invincible. That brings me to my message—"Are we a little like Goliath?" The last thing that was on that giant's mind was being killed. As I thought about Goliath I began to see similarities with my own life. At one time in my life I thought I was invincible, just like Goliath. I took each and every day I had for granted. I thought death was just for older folks. I always figured I would live to be about 80 and pray that will still be true. But I have a much different perspective on life today now that each breath I take is being controlled by a machine. Not long ago I was 35 and invincible. The face of death was the furthest thing from my mind until I was diagnosed with ALS. Up to this point I had taken the very life God had given me for granted. It was truly a wake-up call with my walk with God and how precious each and every day is that we have here on earth.

Before I was diagnosed with ALS I was a fanatic about how my body looked. I would go three to four miles a day on a StairMaster machine five days a week and lift weights at least three days a week. I was in the best shape of my life at the age of 35. To be quite honest, I was pretty proud of the way I looked. On occasion I would even take a quick peek in the mirror to see how all the hard hours in the gym had paid off. I was obsessed with how my body, the flesh, looked. At the peak of my fitness I began to notice twitching in my left arm and asked our ECU trainer about it. He mentioned it was probably no big deal. I was probably fatigued and just needed some rest.

Approximately three months later I was diagnosed with ALS, a disease that attacks the neuromuscular system and, medically speaking, is fatal. At the time of my diagnosis I really didn't have a clue what lay ahead. I suddenly realized the body I was so obsessed with getting to look good didn't seem to matter anymore. The disease slowly began to work its way through my body, starting in my tongue. Yes, my tongue—the one muscle I could care less about how it looked. It went from the tongue to the neck to my left arm and then to my right. Less than a year later, every muscle in my body was affected. Now it is to the point that it is difficult to move from the bed to the bathroom. I basically have no function or the ability to move, other than the little movement I have with my legs, enough that I can walk a little and operate my wheelchair so I can go from place to place with independence.

What's the message from all of this? It brings a significant meaning to who we are and what we're all about. I made a vital mistake that I have been blessed to learn from. That's right. Blessed from ALS, a disease that has taken away the very body I loved. I was obsessed with training all the wrong parts. My flesh was being pushed to the limit, but spiritually I was growing out of shape. The whole time I was thinking my flesh was going to keep me alive, and really it was dying. During this time of seeing my flesh deteriorate I began to devour God's Word, and just the other day I came across this scripture that lifted my spirit. When I read John 6:63 it put it all in perspective. This is Jesus talking to His disciples: "The Spirit gives life; the flesh counts for nothing. The words I have spoken to you are spirit and they are life. "

Right now nobody knows the meaning of this scripture any better than I do. That's the blessing I am talking about that I would have never ever seen. You just don't understand until the very flesh you once were so proud of is taken away. You see, now the only thing I have left is a clear spiritual mind. Each and every day I can continue to grow in God's Word. I no longer worry about exercising the flesh, but instead strive to find that intimate relationship with Jesus. Just as Jesus said, "the flesh counts for nothing and the Spirit is life," we all have one guarantee in life and that is this: Our flesh will die. Whether it's from a disease or old age, it will wilt away. I have gone from a 190-pound body of muscles to about 130 pounds of bones. As weak as my flesh may be, spiritually I am a whole lot stronger than I ever was before. The same kind of effort that it took to get my flesh in shape and to look good is the very same effort required spiritually. If you don't exercise the flesh you will get out of shape. If you don't exercise spiritually you lose sight of life, and you won't realize the flesh counts for nothing.

Not long after I was diagnosed with ALS, September 11th hit. In the midst of trying to figure out the questions of why and how this happened, God began to convict my heart. The reality is that we are searching for all the wrong answers. The truth of the matter is that none of us is invincible. We're a lot like Goliath in sometimes thinking we are. Nobody wakes up thinking they are going to die today, and certainly not one Columbine High School student thought that on the day two young men killed all those students.

Regardless of our age, we are not invincible and nobody knows except God when our last day will be. Does that mean we should live in fear? Absolutely not. Only if you don't have Christ in your life should you fear tomorrow. That was Goliath's whole problem. He had neither love nor respect for God and he thought tomorrow was always going to be there.

So how should we live our lives so we don't become like Goliath? I think I have a unique perspective on this, knowing that any day I could pass, but you know what? I have greater peace today than I ever did before I was diagnosed with ALS—because I have a much better perspective on life. I am not invincible, and I thank God every day for the purpose He has given me. From one day to the next, I don't know what my purpose will be unless I continue to seek Him daily, something I never did before. My pastor, Greg Rogers, asked me a question that really made me think. He said, "What's the difference between happiness and peace? "I thought this was a trick question and then God in His soft voice said, "Happiness doesn't last, but peace does." For 35 years I lived thinking I was invincible and had lots of happiness, but you know what? For the last year and a half I have lived with peace.

As I correlated this story with David and Goliath, I began to notice how David had the peace of God and Goliath had happiness of the flesh. The Bible says God's peace passes all our understanding. What's my point? Don't become like Goliath, thinking you're invincible. Nobody knows the time, day, or hour that will be our last. If we seek God each day for that peace and purpose, it won't matter when that day comes. If we seek each day for happiness, we must realize it can go away. Are we a little bit like Goliath? Only if we don't learn from him.

The flesh of a man is only temporary, but the spirit of a man is life and lives forever and ever. Ask yourself, "How is your flesh?" If the answer is better than your spiritual life, you'd better change your workout program before it's too late. The mirror only reflects what you look like on the outside. Jesus reflects who you are on the inside. We die on the outside and live on the inside. Keep the Word of God flowing throughout you so you can have life and have it more abundantly. Job probably wrote the greatest workout program that nobody ever noticed when he said, "I have treasured His Word more than my daily bread." (cf. Job 23:12b) When bread to feed the flesh becomes the greater desire, always remember that what you're feeding will one day die, and the Word of God will live for eternity.

May God bless this word and grow your spiritual workout program. I pray, God, You will bless these words and allow them to bring glory to Your kingdom.

November 2002
Why?

In conversation with a good friend of mine, the question came up, "Why elect to be put on a vent?" He mentioned that several of his friends couldn't understand going through all of this trouble when I could go be with the Lord. That question brought a stirring of my heart, and I felt compelled to try and answer it. First of all, before this had happened to me, I would have thought the same way those people did: "Why?" But I have learned you can never say you would or would not go on a ventilator until you face that question yourself. It's much easier to say "never" in a hypothetical situation.

What if Paul had said, "I am not going to spend another day in prison. That's it. I quit. Kill me." What would have happened to his witness for God? How about the 13 letters Paul wrote in the New Testament? Most of those letters were written behind prison bars. In the midst of tremendous trials and persecution, God had a powerful calling for Paul's life. The problem in our lives—a lot of the time—is that we think if it doesn't feel good it can't be God. That can be the furthest thing from the truth. Most often it is the exact opposite: It's the persecution we go through that allows us to see God's love. Paul says it best in II Corinthians 12:10, "That is why, for Christ's sake, I delight in weaknesses, in insults, in hardships, in persecutions, in difficulties. For when I am weak, then I am strong." In other words, we would never become strong in Christ without times of strife in our life.

What does this have to do with the question, "Why," in my life? I believe it has tremendous significance in finding the answer. It would have been very easy to give up and pack it in when my health came to the point of being on a ventilator. It could have been a lot easier for my wife Lynn to say, "That's enough," and let go. But God had another plan at that particular time in my life, and it was not to go be with Him. The day Lynn made that decision I was still able to walk; although it was difficult for me to communicate, I still had plenty of life in me. I was just beginning at this point in my life to understand God's love and share Him with others. I had never done that before.

So how could a ventilator improve my testimony for God without the ability to talk? Why would God choose this for anyone? Why did Paul spend so many years in prison? I can't answer those questions with great understanding, but only with trust, the trust that God's plan for our life is far greater than anything we can imagine or fathom. Living God's plan for your life is not always easy, and it requires great persistence.

I can't say living on a ventilator has been easy, and in fact some days I wish I had died, but whenever those thoughts come it never fails—God says something or puts someone in my life that picks me up and moves me forward. Just like with Paul, sometimes God can give us a powerful testimony that we may not be able to see or even understand at that particular point in our life, but in time the message will be revealed. I have never been a writer in my entire life, but I feel this is God's calling for me right now. So the question, "Why?" may never truly be answered at this time. I pray one day that all of these writings may bless somebody, and hopefully lead some lost soldiers to the Lord. I guess that's why I am still alive. I have learned even in the darkest of dark moments Jesus can bring a magnificent light that will uncover the dark. It's never quite as dark as you think it is, unless you don't know Jesus Christ as your personal Savior. May God bless this writing.

October 14, 2004
Above, or Above Average?

The healthiest competition occurs when average people win by putting out above-average effort.

—Colin Powell

I get asked this question frequently: What do you miss most about coaching? I have two very simple answers—the competition and the camaraderie between my coaches, players and managers. My enjoyment of coaching wasn't what I gained personally, but, like Colin Powell said, "win by putting above-average effort." Just seeing a team work so hard and seeing the fruits of their labor pay off was what made coaching to me complete.

We would work the players so hard that they believed no matter who they came up against, they would win. It wasn't like we were the most talented teams, but we certainly put forth an effort second to none and always came into the battles prepared. In fact, I cannot imagine another team outworking us. I am sure every coach says that, but I honestly believed it, and so did our players.

The lessons were never the wins and championships, but rather what went into accomplishing them. That is what I loved about coaching—seeing a group of average young men exceed extraordinary expectations. I don't use the term "average" to be derogatory in anyway, but rather used as a compliment of highest respect. In the end we all learned that it wasn't necessarily the talent, but what was inside the heart that mattered most.

One of my favorite pictures in my coaching career is a framed team picture taken after we put the team through an obstacle course of complete torture. These guys had to snake the football stadium, run around Minges Coliseum, enter the practice soccer field and crawl under barbed wire filled with mud, carry wooden pallets over their head fifty yards, flip tractor tires another fifty yards, and pull a hundred-pound weight to the finish line, not to mention some other crazy stuff in between.

When the guys finished they were covered in mud from head to toe. They all had the look of physical exhaustion on their faces, but deep down, as you look into that team picture you could see an air of self-confidence, like, "I just did something I didn't ever think was possible." Even though they had been pushed beyond their physical and mental limits, it was the challenge and satisfaction of finishing and then turning their attention to their teammates and pushing them to the finish line that seemed to matter most. Because in each player's mind they believed they were leaving the average man behind at the starting line.

Seeing that picture hung on the middle of my wall for years to come. I truly believe it was on that day when those young men turned into champions on the field and, more importantly, developed a belief that they could achieve extraordinary things when they gave an effort above what they thought was possible.

Today when I began to write this, I came across a scripture that I couldn't help but think was the very true meaning of accomplishing extraordinary things. It's in I Corinthians 9:23–24, where the Apostle Paul is speaking to the Corinthian church: "I do all things for the sake of the gospel, so that I may become a fellow partaker of it. Do you know that those who run in a race all run, but only one receives the prize? Run in such a way that you may win." (NASB)

What makes this significant to what Colin Powell was saying is the fact that Paul went through some extremely difficult times to spread the gospel of Christ Jesus. He was not a king of great wealth, but just an average guy, who was touched and called by God. The race wasn't easy on him, but his eyes were focused on the prize (Jesus). Paul was willing to pay the price to win the race and through his great determination, laid a foundation for all of us to follow in receiving Jesus Christ as our championship prize. Just as our teams ran the race for a championship, we all need to be running the race to meet Jesus at the finish line!

Just as I posed the question to our teams, is being average what you want or do you want to be a champion? Of course everyone says champion, but with being a champion comes a significant price tag. I would ask you the same question about your Christian walk. Do you want to be an average disciple of Christ, or do you want to go beyond the call of duty and become extraordinary? If so, are you willing to pay the price? Just think for a second about what Jesus did on the cross. To say we ran a difficult obstacle course in becoming a champion, is nothing in comparison to what Jesus went through on the cross. If you have a hard time understanding how much he suffered for you and me, just watch the movie, *The Passion* and then you will see how much our Heavenly Father truly loves us.

God Bless,
Coach LeClair

November 5, 2004
Unsung Heroes

You can't lead anyone else further than you have gone yourself.
—Gene Mauch

When I was playing college baseball at Western Carolina University, for Jack Leggett, I learned the true meaning of this quote, because I knew Coach would never ask more of me than he was willing to give himself. I had so much respect for this man, and I learned that whether you were a walk-on (like me) or a scholarship player, he was going to demand your very best, just as he would always give his best. I always tried to take this philosophy into my own life and coaching career, hoping to pass it on to others in the same way I learned it from coach Leggett.

I titled this message "unsung heroes," for a particular reason, because throughout my playing and coaching career I have been surrounded by kids who have been an inspiration to me. They were not necessarily the best players—in fact, many of them were walk-ons just like me. But they still made a huge impact on the team and coaches.

I could share many stories with you, but I will just tell about one when I was coaching at Western. I had a young man from New Jersey named Chris who came down to WCU as a walk-on catcher. Chris was a blue-collar kid who worked tremendously hard but didn't get many opportunities to play, because we had an outstanding catcher in front of him. So this young man basically caught pitchers warming up in the bullpens and did all the dirty work nobody else liked to do. He did this for four years and never complained, always answering, yes sir, no sir, trying hard and willingly doing anything to help the team. Whenever we would condition, you could always count on Chris to be up front. In the weight room or on the track, he was always pushing someone else to get better, even though he realized playing time may never come.

I remember one day Chris showed up late for a game with his roommate. I really did not want to punish him, because this was the first time he had ever been late, but his roommate had made a habit out of being not on time. So I decided to run them both in the parking lot for about 30 minutes while the team finished up batting practice. Guess what happened? I forgot they were running and did not realize it until one of my assistants told me after about two and half hours. I sent for them immediately, but only Chris showed up, because the other young man had quit. I walked up to Chris and apologized, as sweat was dripping from his head to toes, but he quickly said, "Coach, it was my fault, and I'm sorry I was late." He immediately walked into the dugout and put his catcher's gear on and went to the bullpen to warm up pitchers.

You see, Chris was an unsung hero. He was an average player, but he had the heart of a lion and he led by example. He was not a super star, but made everyone around him—including myself—better. I would not have traded him for anybody in this world. I loved that kid for who he was and what he stood for.

As I came across this scripture of Peter and John, I thought of Chris and how he helped our team without being the heralded super star, just a courageous unsung hero. Acts 4:13 says: "When they saw the courage of Peter and John and realized that they were unschooled, ordinary men, they were astonished and they took note that these men had been with Jesus."

I have realized through God's word that he used ordinary men, like Peter and John, to do exceptional things. If we learn to have a little more courage and conviction, just think of what we could accomplish. I love the line in this scripture: "They were astonished and they took note that these men had been with Jesus." You see, ordinary men were not supposed to do exceptional things in the Pharisees' eyes, especially not with Jesus. But John, Peter and the rest of Jesus' disciples had lived out Gene Mauch's quote. These men did not just talk the talk, but walked the talk and backed it up with their passion and courage to speak the truth, even though they were ordinary and un-schooled men. Don't you love seeing the courage and con-viction of ordinary men, doing exceptional things beyond human capabilities?

Lord, I thank you for this word and pray that you will challenge us to have more courage in sharing you with others, so that we too may do exceptional things in your name. Let us all be unsung heroes in Jesus' name!

God Bless,
Keith LeClair

November 3, 2004
Scary Moment Turns to Peace

Trust in the Lord with all your heart and lean not on your own understanding; in all your ways acknowledge Him and he will make your paths straight.

—*Proverbs 3:5–6*

In my bathroom on the windowsill, I have this scripture engraved on a round piece of marble where it's in clear view, so I can read it every morning when I get up into my lift and out of bed. As I read it daily I always say, "Lord, this is your day and I trust you with everything that comes my way."

After I got up in my lift yesterday morning to use the bathroom, my trach that connects to my vent popped off just after my nurse left the room. It came off at an angle, where air was still blowing into my trach, so for some reason the vent alarm did not go off to alert the nurse. I looked at my clock on the TV and knew I had about nine minutes before I would see my nurse again.

I was startled and scared all at the same time, and then I began to panic. I began to look around in hopes to catch someone's attention. I could hear Lynn's voice and footsteps in the background, but they soon disappeared into another room. As my eyes turned back around I caught the marble scripture on the windowsill and began just quoting it to myself, "Trust in the Lord with all your heart and lean not on your own understanding," over and over until I felt a tremendous peace. Yes, it was a peace that passes all fleshly understanding. It was me and God in that room, and I knew I was either going to die or live to see another day, so I just lifted it up to the Lord and asked for His will to be done.

About nine minutes had gone by, and I was literally on my last breath, when the nurse walked in and noticed the problem. She quickly hooked up some oxygen, and I quickly started feeling better. I think I was grey and about to pass out when she walked in, and I could see the scared look in her face.

When I finally got in my chair and settled down in front of my Eyegaze, I looked up and thanked God for giving me at least one more day. I know without a shadow of doubt that the scripture on the windowsill saved my life: "Trust in the lord with all your heart and lean not on your own understanding, but in all your ways acknowledge him and he will make your path straight."

I have learned each day my hands and fate are in the hands of God—every second, minute and hour of each day. I do not control my own destiny, but Almighty God. Who are you trusting? What if you were to take your last breath today? Would you have peace that passes all understanding? One day we will all face that day—it is the only fleshly thing I can guarantee—but just remember Jesus is always there, for Jesus Christ is the same yesterday, today and forever (Hebrews 13:8).

God bless,
Keith

December 10, 2004
Jimmy Valvano

Too often we underestimate the power of a touch, a smile, a kind word, a listening ear, an honest compliment, or the smallest act of caring, all of which have the potential to turn a life around.

—Leo Buscaglia

I found this quote months ago, and have been saving it for just the right time. With Christmas just around the corner, you could say now is the right time, but honestly what triggered me to pull this quote up was hearing Jimmy Valvano's speech the other night on ESPN, given right before he passed away nearly 11 years ago.

When Coach V could barely walk up to the podium, taking all the strength he had, I could certainly see and feel through his eyes, because I have traveled down that road before. Once he got to the podium and began to speak, you could see incredible strength and enthusiasm coming from his frail and weakened body.

The more he spoke, the more excited and emotional I got. All I could see as he spoke was the time he and his North Carolina State team won the national championship in 1983 and Coach V was running around the court looking for someone to hug. It was emotional, looking at a vibrant life then, to now seeing a man clinging to life. I guess for the first time I saw and felt what most folks see in me today.

As Jimmy V began to speak, he said you should do three things every day—smile, think and cry—and if you do those three things you will have had a good and full day. As he continued, he had most of the people in the crowd in tears, including myself. It was apparent that Jimmy Valvano loved life, people and God, but most importantly, he loved trying to help others.

When I pulled out this quote from Leo Buscaglia, I couldn't help but see Jimmy Valvano in these words—how many lives he touched and turned around, especially during the last moments of his life. He wasn't down about his cancer. He still had that same enthusiasm in his voice, trying to reach out and touch somebody's life with a smile, caring word or a hug. The last words he spoke on that night were "Don't give up, don't ever give up."

Let me ask you some questions. Is it easier to love your enemies or despise them? Is it easier to get mad at God when trials and tribulations come, or do you praise Him and embrace Him? Is it easier to show patience when you know you're right, or does frustration take over? Is it easier to drive by somebody who has car trouble, or do you stop and help? Is it easier to go to a nursing home and put a smile on someone's face, or to simply say, "I just don't have enough time?"

All these are challenging questions, but each one could change somebody's life. God's word gives a clear understanding of the basic attitudes a disciple is to possess in Luke 10:26–28, when an expert of the law stood up to test Jesus. Jesus quickly asked, him, "What is written in the law?" The expert responded, "Love the Lord your God with all your heart and with all your soul and with all your strength and with all your mind, and love your neighbor as yourself." Jesus replies, "yes you answered correctly."

If we lived this scripture and etched it into our heart, not only would we put a smile on our Heavenly Father's face, but we would certainly impact the lives of so many other people. I would guess that Jesus would fully endorse Leo Buscaglia's quote, and I believe Jesus had a tear and smile on his face that night Jimmy Valvano addressed the crowd at the ESPN Espy Awards.

You know today, not tomorrow, that you could change somebody's life by what you say or do. Wow! What a gift we have, but more importantly, what a gift in sharing the good news of Jesus Christ.

Don't give up, don't ever give up! Thank you, Coach Valvano!

God Bless,

Keith LeClair

May 6, 2005
One Humble Man

Now Moses was a very humble man, more humble than any-one else on the face of the earth.
—Numbers 12:3 (NASB)

Last week, Lynn got a phone call from somebody who wanted to bring Cal Ripken, Jr. by to see me before he spoke to a group here in Greenville. I was actually surprised Lynn knew who Cal Ripken was, because one night Curt Schilling called and I thought she was going to hang up on him, so it's safe to say she has come a long way in recognizing some important baseball names.

I asked Lynn, "What did you say?" She looked at me kind of funny and replied, "What did you think I was going to say, 'No Cal, you can't come?' He'll be here Saturday at 10:15 a.m., but will only be able stay about 15 minutes."

I was so excited, because Cal Ripken, Jr. was one of my heroes growing up, not to mention he is one of the greatest players to ever put on a baseball uniform. You could say I was a tad nervous about meeting him and what I was going to talk about. Heck, here is a guy who broke Lou Gehrig's consecutive game streak of 2,131 games; a record that people thought would never be broken. He also had 3,184 hits and 431 home runs in his career and started in 17 straight All-Star games. I guess we sometimes tend to forget that even the greatest athletes in the world are still human beings just like you and me.

When Saturday finally arrived, he was a little late, and I told Lynn, "He isn't coming." About that time the phone rang and they said they would be here in five minutes, but they were running late and wouldn't be able to stay long. So, I expected the old, "Hello I'm Cal Ripken, and it's nice to meet you" deal, and then *adios amigo*. You know, the big time welcome where you blow in and blow out. Well, that was the farthest thing from the truth when he arrived.

Cal Ripken, Jr was the most humble and grounded person I have ever met. He spent more than an hour with Lynn, Audrey, J.D. and I, just talking baseball and family. If you didn't know his name, you would have never guessed that you were carrying on a conversation with a Hall of Famer.

When I found this verse about Moses this morning I couldn't help but think of Cal Ripken, Jr. No, I'm not comparing Cal to Moses or anything close to that. For that matter, I don't even know if Cal Ripken, Jr. is even a Christian. But the comparison you could draw between the two is that, like Moses, he was a very humble man, and I couldn't see anyone in our sports profession today that could be any more humble or grounded than Cal Ripken, Jr.

After about an hour, we got Cal to take a family picture with us and sign four or five baseballs. J.D, of course, was a little wiggle worm who couldn't sit still and was probably trying to show off for our guest. But, what was great was that Cal laughed at him and said, "You remind me of my son," and then proceeded to wrestle with him.

I learned a couple of valuable lessons from this visit. One, you can't judge a man by his success or fame. Secondly, a humble man has a chance to really impact so many lives by just giving of his time and being down to earth. You know something, Cal Ripken, Jr. made a huge impression on me and he left not even knowing what he did.

Are you humble with others regardless of who they may be, or do you treat somebody differently depending on their status? A humble heart is one that has compassion for others that are less fortunate! So, my word for today is to humble yourself before our Lord and Savior, Jesus Christ, who was so humble he was crucified for you and me.

God Bless,
Keith LeClair

January 17, 2005
What's the Prize?

The last year I was head baseball coach at East Carolina University, I had perhaps the best team in the 11 years that I coached. I mean, we could do it all! We hit, pitched, played great defense and had good team speed to run the base paths. As a team, we literally crushed most of our opponents. Above all, we had tremendous team chemistry, with everyone working towards our ultimate prize—the College World Series. By season's end, we were ranked in the top fifteen in the country and had everyone talking about a chance to make it all the way to the College World Series. The College World series is equivalent to the Final Four in basketball, and it had been a personal goal of mine dating way back to 1985 when I was a freshman on the Western Carolina Baseball team.

I was still pursuing this goal (or better called obsession) 16 years later, at East Carolina University in 2001. This became the last team I coached at East Carolina University due to my diagnosis of ALS; even though I continued to coach one more season, I was struggling with the disease and did very little coaching. My assistant coaches ran the show, so I really refer to the 2001 season as my last.

As you can tell, my life was consumed with the prize of winning baseball games. I can't explain the high I got from competing and winning games. All I can tell you is that winning was like an addiction for me. I spent most of my time in life figuring out how to get an edge so I could win my next game. At times, (well, a lot of times) my wife and kids took a back seat to my prize, but most importantly, I didn't have time for God. Looking back, that's what hurts me the most, not putting God and my family first. I can't say God wasn't using me to mold young men and help them to understand doing the right things, because I now can see His hand was upon me and working all the time.

As for my family, they truly seemed to be the ones having to take the back seat for an obsession of winning, especially my wife. It's not easy being a wife and raising two kids alone most of the time, having to sacrifice for your husband's obsession so he could succeed. If it were not for Lynn today, I would be all alone and would have never even gotten my prize of winning it all.

Before I make my point, I must go back to the 2001 season. That year we had an older team that the coaching staff had been molding to achieve our ultimate goal of getting to the College World Series. The previous two seasons we had been knocking on the door, but we just couldn't seem to get the breaks to get to our final destination. But this season seemed different, and I just knew in my heart that this was the year. As the season went on, everything was falling into place. By season's end, we had won more than 40 games and were selected as one of the top eight national seeds in the country. This seeding allowed us to host one of 16 Regionals around the country. The 16 winners could move on and play in the Super Regionals, with the eight winners advancing to the College World Series.

After hosting and winning the regional tournament in three straight games, we now were among 16 teams left in the country. Next were the Super Regionals, and our opponent was the University of Tennessee. Whoever won two of three games would move on to Omaha, Nebraska, and play in the College World Series. This is when God opened my eyes to the true "ultimate prize." After two heartbreaking losses to Tennessee I stood in the outfield and comforted my players. I thought, "OK, God. What do you want me to tell these young men?" I spoke these words without having any idea that this would be the last time I ever put on a baseball uniform. I brought the team in real close and with tears rolling down my cheeks, I said, "Men, if losing this game is the worst thing that ever happens to you in your lifetime, you are going to have a great life." After I said that, we took a knee as a team and prayed the Lord's Prayer.

What makes those words so significant was the fact that two weeks later I was diagnosed with ALS. I believe God was speaking to me, and using that opportunity to build and put priorities in those young men's lives. Over the next week I also believe God told me I was good enough to achieve that prize of going to the College World Series, but He had a better prize for me than that. He told me I was good enough when two of the top programs in the country called me to interview for their coaching vacancies. As I look back on those two situations, I feel God was protecting me like never before. Both job opportunities never really felt right in my heart, and two weeks later I was diagnosed with ALS.

So even when you seem to be walking through the darkest valley of your life, God is always there. What I learned and hope to help you realize through this message is that it is very easy for all of us to get caught up with chasing the wrong prize. For me, it was the obsession of winning and achieving certain goals. I think all of us are driven by something other than what God tells us. I came across this verse in Philippians and it brought this message out to me. Just hear the words and repeat them to yourself several times. The verses are Phil. 3:13–14: "Brethren, I do not regard myself as having laid hold of it yet; but one thing I do: forgetting what lies behind and reaching forward to what lies ahead." (NASB)

As I look at that verse, I clearly see that my life was never looking ahead but only holding onto what was behind. I was chasing after a prize that would only last a moment. Now let's read verse 14: "I press on toward the goal for the prize of the upward call of God in Christ Jesus." (NASB) God's word tells us there is only one prize that will be everlasting.

All my trophies that I won will one day rust away and no longer have any meaning. The dream house you worked so hard to get one day won't be standing. All the hours you worked to accumulate millions one day won't matter. All the goals and prizes we strive for in our lifetime will absolutely have no significance in our lives unless we put the prize of Jesus Christ first. You know when God told me my prize didn't matter? When I spoke those last words to my team. I should have just as well read Phil 3:13–14 to them, because truly that was what I was trying to say on that day. My priorities have changed dramatically over the last couple of years since my diagnosis of ALS. Many of you may need to get your focus off your own prize and lock your eyes on the greatest prize of all, our Lord and Savior, Jesus Christ.

March 10, 2005
Anger

"In your anger do not sin": Do not let the sun go down while you are still angry." (Ephesians 4:26)

For man's anger does not bring about the righteous life that God desires. (James 1:20)

I wish throughout my life that I could honestly say I had upheld the words of these two scriptures, but unfortunately I cannot. I can say, though, that over time my ability to handle and control anger has become much better with the help of God.

I don't think anybody can look at themselves in a mirror and say they have never sinned from their anger. I would bet we all have at some point in our lives, and most of us have probably even taken that anger to bed with us and woke up still angry the next morning.

I know in my 11-year head coaching career I got so angry at times I took it out on umpires and occasionally my players, especially when I first became a head coach. During those years I gained the reputation of being a hothead who argued every call. What I really regret about those times was the way I displayed my conduct.

I remember on one occasion during my first year at ECU as a head coach, we were playing Campbell at their field when the umpire, Ron Sebastian, made what I thought was a bad call. Well, to make the story short, I went berserk and got thrown out of the game. It was a close game that we eventually lost, and I felt I had let the team down. Even worse, I had let myself down.

When I look back on that night, I see that God taught me a valuable lesson that has forever changed my life. I finally had my eyes and heart opened to the fact, that I was not only letting my behavior put a mark on me, but I wasn't setting a very good Christian example for my players or anyone else who was in attendance at that game.

I remembering riding back on the bus that night filled with regret and embarrassment over what had taken place. I began to seek God after this incident and pray for forgiveness and for more of a peaceful spirit. I can actually say from that point on I handled myself in a different manner with umpires. I won't lie and say I never argued with umpires again, but I will say I didn't take my anger out on them.

You know, for the longest time I carried the guilt of that particular night with me, until I saw the umpire, Ron Sebastian, at a fall league game in Raleigh. I remember that day like it was yesterday. He was standing behind the backstop taking in the game, when I walked up to him and apologized. I told him the incident had been on my mind for a long time and that I really felt bad over the way I conducted myself. He pulled me off to the side and talked to me a long while, and to this day I believe that moment changed me as a coach and more importantly strengthened my walk with Christ. He mentored to me and just said some things that really hit home to me that day, which lifted a tremendous guilt off my shoulders. I realized that my anger not only hurt him but was eating me up inside and out.

I truly have a better understanding of what God is trying to tell us in these two scriptures, and hopefully you will as well. First, you can't avoid anger sometimes, but what you can do is learn how to handle and control it. If we don't, eventually it will lead to sin and bring us to do things we normally would not, which God truly wants us to avoid. Second, it's important to recognize your anger and seek God for forgiveness, before the anger builds to a boiling point of destruction.

For me personally, I know that when I feel guilt and

remorse, that's God talking to me and it's time to let go and apologize to whoever or whatever it is you're angry at. Just think, if the world applied these two scriptures to everyday life, what a more peaceful and safe world we would live in. So, before the sun goes down, let go of your anger and when the sun comes up, ask God for a peaceful spirit.

I am afraid anger is one of the biggest road barriers we deal with daily in having a more intimate and open relationship with our Lord and Savior, Jesus Christ. God cannot use an angry spirit to show others his love! Lord knows, it took my stubborn personality a while to figure this out.

God Bless,
Keith LeClair

August 22, 2005
Gethsemane

Then Jesus went with his disciples to a place called Gethse-
mane, and he said to them, "Sit here while I go over there and
pray." He took Peter and the two sons of Zebedee along with
him, and he began to be sorrowful and troubled. Then he said
to them, "My soul is overwhelmed with sorrow to the point of
death. Stay here and keep watch with me."
Going a little farther, he fell with his face to the ground
and prayed, "My Father, if it is possible, may this cup be taken
from me. Yet not as I will, but as you will."

—Matthew 26:36–39

OK, you're sound asleep and all of the sudden you get a
tap on your shoulder at about 4 a.m. You roll over and say,
"Who's there? And it better be good." "Hey Billy Bob, it's
me, God. I am sorry to inform you, but I am here to say
that you only have one more day to live."

What would you do? Roll back over and fall asleep, or
would you spring out of bed and fall to your knees and cry
out to God? Jesus, our Lord and Saviour, was basically confronted with almost this exact situation. The Son of God,
right before he was going to be captured by the Roman soldiers and carried off and crucified on the cross for our sins,
went off to a quiet place and prayed. If that doesn't bring
tears to your eyes, nothing will. Jesus wasn't just praying to
his Father for himself, but for all who believed in him.

I remember when I was first told by a doctor that I had
ALS. I immediately went home and fell on my knees and
cried out to God. I have no idea what I said; all I could
feel—for the first time in my life—was that I was totally
helpless and completely in the hands of God. Although
God didn't tell me that I had one more day to live, it sure
felt as if He did.

Over the past four years I have tried to live as if I only

had one more day, because truly I am on the edge of death daily. I get up every morning and thank God for all the blessings He has provided me, and then I pray for my family and others who have special needs that God has laid on my heart. But, most importantly I pray seeking his purpose and plan for my life that day, and that His will be done. What's amazing, through this ongoing battle with ALS, is that when I was perfectly healthy I only prayed and called on God when my family or I was in need. Pretty selfish, wasn't it? Oh, how things change when you think you have "one more day."

What I have learned is that when you think you have—or truly only have—"one more day" in your life, what matters most is your relationship with Jesus and your family. All of a sudden your job, money, house, and possessions have very little meaning or value. But crying out to God, hugging your kids and wife and being with your family dominate your thoughts 24 hours a day, seven days a week. Those things you take for granted, I promise you, are priceless.

I get this question asked to me a lot: "Why do you keep pushing on, wanting to live like this?" I often think about this very question myself. The answer I can give is that God truly uses you when you're at the weakest point. When you almost think another step or breath, or in my case just one more blink of the eye, is impossible, that is when God steps in and uses you to your fullest spiritual potential. When Paul wrote in II Corinthians 12:10, "For when I am weak, then I am strong," he was certainly speaking the truth!

If I could teach everyone one lesson from this lengthy fight with Lou Gehrig's Disease it would be this: "Live your life like you have 'one more day' and tell your family how much you love them every day." Falling on your knees in front of God isn't a weakness, but a strength.

God bless,
Keith LeClair

COLOPHON

DESIGN

Book designed by Whitecaps Media

Main body composed in Minion Pro; devotional section
    composed in Scala Sans

Cover designed by Lisa Stroud

PHOTO CREDITS

Courtesy of East Carolina Media Relations:
    cover, viii, 3, 39, 42, 50, 53, 76, 78, 84, 95, 126, 140, 142, 149,
    back cover

Courtesy of Doris LeClair: 8, 9, 18, 35

Courtesy of Western Carolina University Media Relations:
    30, 103 (photos by Mark Haskett)

Courtesy of *The Daily Reflector*: 119, 123
    (photos by Rhett Butler)

Courtesy of Michelle Mazey: 105

Courtesy of Nick Schnabel: 131

ABOUT THE AUTHOR

BETHANY BRADSHER has been covering East Carolina athletics for the past ten years and has been a journalist since 1990. In 1995 as a sportswriter for the Spartanburg *Herald-Journal*, she covered the inaugural two seasons of the Carolina Panthers and the preparations for the 1996 Summer Olympics in Atlanta. She has written for the Associated Press, the Durham *Herald-Sun*, the Orlando *Sentinel,* and the Houston *Post*, as well as several magazines. *Coaching Third* is her first book.

She and her husband Sid live in Greenville, North Carolina, with their four children.